The Politics and Strategy of the Second World War
edited by Noble Frankland and Christopher Dowling

BURMA
1942–1945

RAYMOND CALLAHAN

BURMA
1942-1945

NEWARK
University of Delaware Press

Copyright© 1978 by Raymond Callahan
Introduction copyright© 1978
by Noble Frankland and Christopher Dowling
DO NOT USE

FIRST AMERICAN EDITION PUBLISHED 1979

Associated University Presses, Inc.
Cranbury, New Jersey 08512

Library of Congress Catalogue Card Number: 79-52240
ISBN 0-87413-162-6

PRINTED IN THE UNITED STATES OF AMERICA

TO SARAH AND BRIAN

CONTENTS

ACKNOWLEDGEMENTS

Unlike previous volumes in this series, the present work covers the entire war in a particular theatre, and the author is very conscious of the debt he owes to the Official Histories, those indispensable trail blazers. I would also like to acknowledge gratefully the assistance of the Public Record Office, the Imperial War Museum, and the Liddell Hart Centre for Military Archives at King's College. Lieutenant-General Sir Ian Jacob, GBE, CB, gave me the benefit not only of his stimulating conversation but of his diary of the Casablanca conference, and Lieutenant-General Sir Reginald Savory, KCIE, CB, DSO, MC, very kindly answered a number of queries about the reorganization of training in the Indian Army in 1943. I am deeply indebted to Mr Ronald Lewin, Field-Marshal Lord Slim's official biographer, for a lengthy and enlightening discussion of the war in Burma, as well as for generously making his book available to me in typescript. The series' editors were unfailingly helpful and sympathetic. My colleague and friend George Basalla read the manuscript with a critical eye, while, without the kindness and hospitality of Bill and Ann Reader, an American scholar would have found the task of working in London far more onerous. Needless to say, I am responsible for the conclusions drawn.

EDITORS' INTRODUCTION

Numerous books and articles have been written about the weapons, battles, and campaigns of the Second World War, and the problems of command, supply and intelligence have been extensively surveyed. Yet, though the fighting has been so fully described from these and other angles, the reasons why the various military operations took place have attracted less study and remain comparatively obscure. It is to fill this gap in the understanding of the Second World War that this series of monographs has been conceived.

The perceptive have always understood the extent to which war is a continuation of policy by other means, and the clash of armies or fleets has, in intention, seldom been haphazard. Battles and campaigns often contain the keys to the understanding of the grand strategies of supreme commands and the political aims and purpose of nations and alliances.

In each of the volumes in this series an important battle or campaign is assessed with the object of discovering its relationship to the war as a whole, for in asking the question Why was this battle fought? and What effect did it produce? one is raising the issue of the real meaning and character of the war.

Among the volumes published at the outset of the series have been studies from this fundamental point of view of the Russo-Finnish campaign of 1939-1940, the campaign in France and Belgium in 1940, the campaign in Iraq and Syria in 1941 and the German invasion of Russia.

In the volume on Finland, Anthony Upton has shown how the fighting there provided both the Allies and the Germans with a pretext for intervening in Scandinavia and led directly to the Norwegian campaign. He also shows how Britain, France and Germany were led to under-estimate the Soviet military potential to an extent which was nearly fatal to Britain and which, in the event, was ruinous to Germany.

In his study of the campaign in France and Belgium Brian Bond demonstrates that the sweeping German victory was due not only to a superiority of military tactical doctrine but also to the disparate strategies and politics of the three allies.

On Iraq and Syria, Geoffrey Warner exposes Hitler's lost opportunity of securing oil supplies and perhaps of inflicting on

Britain a disaster in the Middle East comparable to that which the Japanese inflicted on her in the Far East. Although the loss of Egypt and the Middle Eastern oilfields would not necessarily have brought about Britain's defeat, the war would certainly have been considerably prolonged.

Robert Cecil examines the background to Hitler's fatal decision to invade Russia, which not only made it inevitable that Germany would be defeated but ensured that the balance of power in postwar Europe would be fundamentally altered. He argues that Barbarossa was launched not for cogent military reasons but in order to gratify Hitler's long-cherished racial and ideological obsessions, which also dictated the manner in which the campaign was waged.

As the series progresses, its readers, advancing case by case, will be able to make general judgements about the central character of the Second World War. Some will find this worthwhile in its own right; others will see it as a means of increasing their grasp of the contemporary scene. More than thirty years have passed since the death of Hitler and the capitulation of Japan. These momentous events were the culmination of a war which transformed the political and social, the economic and technological and, indeed, the general conditions of society and politics in virtually every corner of the world.

NOBLE FRANKLAND: CHRISTOPHER DOWLING

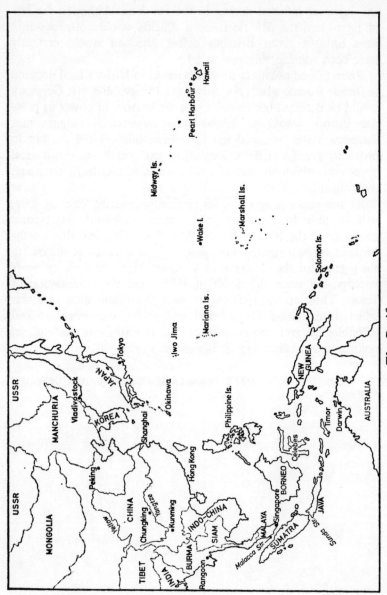

The Pacific 1942–1945

I

Prelude to Disaster: 1937-1941

On board the *Queen Mary*, ploughing westward across the Atlantic in May 1943, Winston Churchill composed a paper on Britain's contribution to the war against Japan, which he knew would be a major item on the agenda of the fifth Anglo-American summit conference of the war. Much of the paper was taken up by discussion of Burma, where recent events had been very unsatisfactory – so much so that the Prime Minister was prepared to close it down as an active theatre. 'Going into swampy jungles to fight the Japanese is like going into the water to fight a shark,' he commented, and went on to propose an amphibious strategy that would bypass Burma. 'It should be possible to carry up to thirty thousand or forty thousand men across the Bay of Bengal, as required, to one or more points of the crescent from Moulmein to Timor . . .'[1] In fact the British would fight on in Burma for the duration of the war, the bold amphibious strategy that Churchill sought doomed, by the imperatives of alliance politics, to remain a tantalizing but insubstantial dream. The primacy of politics over strategy is nowhere better illustrated than in Britain's war against Japan. Although Burma was the focus of that war, the campaign there cannot be understood without a retrospective glance at the development of British strategy in the Far East in the years before Japan struck.

The incompatibility between Britain's interest in the Far Eastern status quo and Japan's ambitions was evident before 1914, and the Admiralty was considering the possibility of a future war with Japan by 1917. The decision to abrogate the Anglo-Japanese alliance, taken under American and dominion pressure in 1921, therefore found the naval staff prepared with a strategy for an Anglo-Japanese war. It required a major fleet base in the Far East, and posited the ability to move the bulk of the Royal Navy's capital ships east to meet any Japanese attack. Singapore was chosen as the site for the base, after Hong Kong had been ruled out as too exposed and Australia as too remote. A fleet based at

Singapore would cover the entrance to the Indian Ocean and would be in a position on the flank of any Japanese thrust southward towards Australia and New Zealand. That a fleet would be available was an assumption that gradually hardened into dogma because without a fleet the construction of the base, indeed the entire strategy, became absurd. But the possibility of actually sending any sizeable fleet east had begun to fade almost at the moment the strategy pivoting on that fleet had become official policy. Unfortunately, the 1922 Washington Treaties on naval limitation, shaped largely by American wishes, had restricted the British to a navy equal to meeting commitments in one hemisphere, but not simultaneously a world-wide Empire's. Britain's post-war financial situation and the general mood of the country would probably have produced much the same result even without the treaties. From 1922 Britain's Far Eastern empire was in fact defenceless, unless the Japanese obligingly attacked at a moment of profound European tranquillity. Exactly the opposite was the more likely occurrence, as the naval staff itself had pointed out in December 1920. British strategy in the Far East was based from the beginning on bluff and self-deception. Yet there seemed no alternative to the hollow Singapore strategy except a public recognition that Britain's eastern interests were indefensible and a renunciation of responsibility for anything beyond India. While logical, such a renunciation was as impossible politically as building the fleet necessary to put teeth into the official policy. The receding tide of British power and will had left Britain's eastern interests, as well as the British commitment to defend the Pacific dominions, hostages to fortune.[2]

Were there any alternatives open to the British government that might have offered a better chance of defending the eastern empire against Japan? Some Whitehall policymakers regretted the breach with Japan and believed that the easiest way out of the resulting dilemma was to recognize that a mistake had been made and to seek a rapprochement with Japan. In the early thirties Neville Chamberlain, then Chancellor of the Exchequer, Sir Warren Fisher, the Permanent Under-Secretary at the Treasury, and Sir Robert Vansittart, who held the same position at the Foreign Office, all flirted with the idea, which would have saved money and allowed undivided concentration on the growing menace of Germany. Whether such a rapprochement would have been possible on any terms the British could have accepted is doubtful, but the obstacle to even trying was that any such attempt would be seen in Washington as anti-American, and the resulting cost for Britain might be very high. On the eve of the Second London Naval Conference (December 1935-March 1936), Franklin Roosevelt cabled the American representative, Norman Davis, telling him to warn the supposed 'pro-Japanese' faction in the British government that 'if Great Britain is even suspected of preferring to play with Japan to playing with us' he would 'approach public sentiment' in the dominions to make them 'understand clearly that their future security is linked with us.'[3] This rather breathtaking threat to take the dominions away from Britain may have been largely bluff, but the fact that it was even made reveals the underlying tension in Anglo-American relations, which were really quite bad in the twenties and only improved very gradually thereafter. British policymakers had decided before 1914 that, for reasons pragmatic as well as sentimental, hostilities with the United States were out of the question, and Asquith's government had instructed the Admiralty not to consider America as a possible opponent. (The United States Navy, by contrast, had a plan, 'Red', for war against Britain ready as late as 1934, as well as another plan, 'Red-Orange', to meet an Anglo-Japanese combination.) Since the British had assumed a unilateral obligation to maintain good relations with the United States, major disputes could end only with concessions to the American viewpoint. The most consistent British exercise in appeasing a foreign rival can be seen in the course of Anglo-American relations after 1918.

If an Anglo-Japanese rapprochement was ruled out by American hostility to Japan, was an Anglo-American understanding based on the threat Japan posed to both powers an alternative? There is little doubt that many British policymakers hoped for something like this, but arrangements, even informal, with Britain were not something that had any appeal to the America of Harding, Coolidge, Hoover or the pre-1940 Roosevelt. The Japanese threat to British and American interests in China, which became acute with the outbreak of hostilities between China and Japan in 1937, made little real difference to this distant American attitude. The United States supported the Chinese government, but the Roosevelt administration, wary of provoking outbursts from isolationists, or traditionally anti-British groups of Democratic voters like the Irish-Americans, resolutely opposed a joint Anglo-American diplomatic front against the Japanese. Roosevelt made vague references to a 'naval quarantine' of Japan in his speech at Chicago on 5 October 1937, and subsequently sent Captain Royal Ingersoll to London for confidential talks with the Admiralty in January 1938. Nothing came of Ingersoll's mission, however, except agreements on areas of responsibility, and on the exchange of codes and communications personnel once a war with Japan had broken out, whereas the British by that time desperately needed help in *preventing* a war in the Far East. In fact, the British got the worst of all worlds as far as their relations with Japan and America were concerned. Debarred from even exploring a rapprochement with Japan because of American views, they remained nevertheless uncertain about the degree of American support they could expect if a breach with Japan occurred, while the attempt to stay in step with the Americans increased the likelihood of a break. There was little the British could do except to hope that whatever happened, happened to them and the Americans together.[4]

British helplessness in the Far East was underlined by events in Europe. Although the Singapore strategy was ritually reaffirmed at the last pre-war Imperial Conference in May 1937, the deteriorating European situation was forcing British planners to alter their strategy to conform to reality, and that reality was that Britain's national existence could only be threatened by Germany, not by Japan. Captain T. S. V. Phillips, the Admiralty's Director of Plans, told Ingersoll in January 1938 that nine capital ships, three carriers and 19 cruisers would form the core of the fleet sent to Singapore, but he carefully added that the outbreak of a war in Europe would scale this force down considerably.[5] The events of the ensuing year made a general European war much more likely, and by February 1939 the Director of Military Operations at the War Office, Major-General Henry Pownall, was noting in his diary that the Navy had become very cautious about the size of the force that could be sent to Singapore, and had increased the time required for it to get there from seventy to ninety days.[6] In June 1939 the Admiralty's caution had become even more marked and 'main fleet to Singapore' had dwindled to a carrier and a battlecruiser to be based on Ceylon for trade protection in the Indian Ocean. When war came in September the 'period before relief', the time Singapore was expected to hold out on its own, was doubled, to 180 days. Pownall had observed in February that Singapore's sliding priority would seriously disturb Australia and New Zealand – if they knew.[7] He acutely put his finger on a very awkward fact. A gap opened up after 1937 between what the British realized they had to do, and what they had assured the Pacific dominions for years that they would do. While British strategy changed under the pressure of events, official priorities remained unaltered. On 8 December 1941 Singapore still ranked second only to the United Kingdom itself – in theory.

The most important fact in the alteration of Britain's strategic priorities was the rise of the Mediterranean as a focus of political and strategic concern, and a possible theatre of offensive activity. The disintegration of the Singapore strategy really began in the Mediterranean, with the Abyssinian crisis that led to the breach with Italy. The fleet for the Far East was to come in the first instance from the Mediterranean, and through that sea lay the shortest route for warships, troop convoys, and supplies on their way east. Italy's hostility deranged plans for moving the fleet east and posed as well a threat to the extensive British interests in the eastern Mediterranean and Arab world. When Britain finally accepted the inevitability of a 'continental commitment', the views and opinions of the French, to whom the Mediterranean as the link with their African empire and its armies was a matter of primary importance, became an important determinant of British policy. The decision taken in the spring of 1939 to try to block further German expansion east or south deepened British commitments in the eastern basin of the Mediterranean. When war came the only serious offensive plans the Anglo-French alliance had were for a Mediterranean offensive against Italy, and the British had begun to develop the Egyptian base area that would sustain the coming years of fighting. The Mediterranean, despite the anticlimax of Italian neutrality, had quietly dispossessed the Far East as the British empire's first priority after the home islands themselves, a development that, in turn, had a major impact on the empire's strategic reserve, the Indian Army.[8]

The Indian Army had been reorganized in 1922-23 to incorporate some of the lessons of World War I and, in particular, to overcome some of the weaknesses that became apparent in 1914-15 when that army had to be expanded rapidly and maintained in theatres far distant from its recruiting grounds in India. Ironically, in March 1921 the Indian Legislative Assembly had defined the Indian Army's duties as the defence of India's frontiers and the maintenance of internal security, thus apparently undercutting its role as the empire's strategic reserve. In the political climate of 1921, with the 1919 Government of India Act fresh on the statute book, the Viceroy and his advisers and Whitehall had little option but to accept this definition. Throughout the twenties, the Indian Army's energies, when not occupied by 'aid to the civil' or tribal skirmishes on the North-West Frontier, were directed solely toward planning the defence of that frontier against Russia until the arrival of reinforcements from the United Kingdom. There was something a bit unreal about this exercise, since a Russian attack through Afghanistan was highly improbable. Furthermore, imperial defence policy for nearly a century past had hinged on the ready availability of Indian troops as a freely disposable strategic reserve, and this role had become more, not less, significant as a result of the growth of British commitments in the Middle East after 1919. In 1929 the War Office asked India to agree to the dispatch of three brigade groups to protect the oilfields of Persia and Iraq, as well as the Persian Gulf ports, in the event of a Russian attack on the Middle East. Even before the Mediterranean and Middle East became a determinant in British strategic planning, it was designated as the Indian Army's most probable area of overseas operations.

Concurrently with the evolution of the 1935 Government of India Act, the Garran Tribunal (1933) investigated India's role in imperial defence, and reaffirmed the 1921 definition of the Indian Army's mission. At the same time, however, the role of imperial strategic reserve was officially resurrected and a grant of £1,500,000 from the Exchequer to India was agreed to support preparations for overseas activity by the Indian Army. Over the next four years, India agreed to send a brigade to Singapore and the remainder of the Fourth Indian division to the Middle East, and accepted much more qualified commitments to aid in the defence of Hong Kong and Burma. Despite the Garran Tribunal's affirmation of India's imperial reserve role, these agreements remained closely guarded secrets because they might have been very embarrassing politically in the climate of the early thirties. They are in fact an interesting commentary on the 1935 Act, since clearly British planners assumed that, whatever political changes were agreed, the Indian Army would remain, in part at least, at their disposal. The assumption was easier to make since without that army the defence of the empire's interests east of Suez, already very difficult, would become impossible.

If, however, the Indian Army was to function as a reserve for the British position in the Middle East, major changes in its structure and organization were urgently necessary. Superbly professional though it was, the Indian Army was ill-equipped to fight a first class power – it had no armoured units of its own, for example, and its twenty cavalry regiments were still largely horsed. In October 1938 a Modernization Committee, chaired by Major-General C. J. E. Auchinleck, recommended extensive mechanization – a prerequisite for war in the Middle East, among other things. Auchinleck almost immediately thereafter became the Indian Army member of the commission headed by Admiral of the Fleet Lord Chatfield that had arrived in India to conduct a review of India's role in imperial defence. On 30 January 1939, the commission signed its report in Delhi. The commitments undertaken piecemeal since 1933 were formalized into an obligation to maintain a force of External Defence Troops, equipped on a higher scale than the rest of the Indian Army, ready to proceed overseas to bolster the defences of the Middle East and Singapore, which were defined as bastions of India's security – thus neatly bringing the imperatives of imperial defence within the 1921 and 1933 definitions of the Indian Army's role, and making the whole business more defensible to Indian political opinion. The Chatfield commission also recommended the mechanization and modernization of the whole Indian Army over a five-year period, with material and funding being supplied by the United Kingdom. The last point was crucial since, in 1938, India was spending 57 percent of its central government revenue on defence (the comparable figure for the United Kingdom itself was 27 percent) – a proportion bound to come under increasing challenge by Indian opinion. Chamberlain's War Cabinet accepted the Chatfield Report on 5 September 1939, agreeing to supply equipment and technical specialists as well as £30 million to modernize the Indian Army. By that time the 4th Indian Division, the External Defence Force, had left India, one brigade going to Singapore and the rest of the division to the Middle East, taking with it virtually the entire Indian reserve stock of modern weapons and vehicles.[9]

The Indian Army was committed to the Middle East because of the importance the area assumed in the late thirties in the eyes of policymakers in London who were still, political changes notwithstanding, in a position to dispose of India's military resources. This orientation was assisted by the traditional concern of the Government of India with keeping hostile European powers out of the Middle East, and last but not least, by India's dependence on the United Kingdom for the necessary finance and supply to modernize its army, which meant that London's perceptions would shape the Indian Army's capabilities. In all this, defence against Japan did not figure. The dispatch of the 12th Indian Infantry Brigade to Singapore in August 1939 was intended merely to bolster the local defence of the 'fortress' whose real security was deemed to reside in its fixed defences, a scanty provision of aircraft, and a fleet that the British government knew could not be sent. The defence of India's north-east frontier was never actively considered in London or Delhi during the interwar years because the arrival of an enemy there seemed such a remote possibility. Few Indian – or British – army officers had the foresight of Lieutenant-Colonel W. J. Slim, who, while commanding the 2/7th Gurkha Rifles in Assam in 1938, had exercised his men in jungle combat against an imaginary Japanese invading force. The Japanese, in any case not a 'first class opponent' in most western eyes, would be blocked by the Navy, the RAF and the Singapore fortress – meanwhile, the Indian Army could concentrate on modernizing, expanding, and preparing for real war in the Middle East.

The decision to concentrate on the Middle East was reinforced by the events of May-June 1940. The French collapse and the Italian entry into the war stripped away the last shreds of pretence that Britain could defend its eastern empire. Menaced by invasion, the United Kingdom was fighting for survival. Anything that did not directly contribute to that end had to be ignored. Malaya's tin and rubber earned vital dollars to pay for

North American supplies, and the authorities there were ordered to allow nothing, even defence preparations, to interfere with maximum output. At the same time the Pacific dominions were informed, on 13 June, of the official demise of the Singapore strategy and told that in the absence of a British fleet in the Far East, London was looking to America to restrain Japan – they were not, however, told that there was no sign the United States would perform the role for which it was cast. On 3 July 1940 the commanders-in-chief in the Middle East and India were informed that despite the strategic revolution the Middle East would be defended as long as possible.

A long war of attrition was all the British Chiefs of Staff could offer amid the catastrophe of May 1940 as a strategy for ultimate victory, and in such a struggle it would be very important to deny Germany and Italy the oil of the Middle East and, if possible, the raw materials of the Balkans. Only in the Mediter-ranean could the British now hope to operate offensively against the weaker of the Axis powers. Finally, expulsion or withdrawal from the Middle East would have been a psychological blow whose magnitude, coming after the German conquest of western Europe, would have been serious, if not fatal, especially to Churchill's hopes of coaxing a steadily growing volume of sup-port out of the United States. Britain itself, re-equipping its army after Dunkirk and bracing to meet an invasion attempt, needed more than ever to draw on the dominions and India to build up an army capable of holding the Middle East. Australia and New Zealand, however, both with troops already in Egypt, were concerned about their own security now that Britain could not send a fleet, while Japan's ability to strike south had been enhanced by the vulnerability of French Indochina to penetra-tion. In a paper for the War Cabinet the vice-chiefs of staff pointed out on 4 July 1940 that unless they were satisfied about their own security, the Pacific dominions were unlikely to send more men overseas, and amid the accelerating air battle over Britain a new strategy was cobbled together to provide at least the illusion of security in the Far East. Reverting to the argu-ments advanced by Sir Hugh Trenchard, the Chief of the Air Staff, in the twenties, the strategy articulated by the Chiefs of Staff in a massive paper of 8 August proposed to make the RAF Malaya's first line of defence, supplemented by a large garrison to hold the entire peninsula while the RAF was brought up to a strength of twenty-one squadrons with 336 first line aircraft. Whether this strategy would have worked is problematic, but in fact it was never tried. Neither the troops nor the planes could be, or at any rate were, made available. Its existence on paper, however, smoothed the task of extracting men for the Middle East from Australia and New Zealand.

The creation of a new command structure in the Far East marked the adoption of an air power strategy to replace the defunct concept of 'main fleet to Singapore'. Air Chief Marshal Sir Robert Brooke-Popham, a distinguished but elderly and once-retired officer, was named Commander-in-Chief, Far East, in October 1940. He was given an inadequate staff, incomplete authority over the army and RAF, none over the navy (which controlled his principal source of intelligence) or the various civil authorities, and responsibility for the immense arc from Burma to Hong Kong, as well as for liaison with the Dutch and Americans in the Far East. Burma became part of Brooke-Popham's command despite the Government of India's request for operational control there. The Indian authorities argued that Burma was a defensive bastion for eastern India, especially the important industrial area around Calcutta, and that Burma would look to India for reinforcements in any case. The decision to include Burma in Brooke-Popham's unwieldy command had little to do with the intractable problem of defence against Japan, however, but was determined by a factor of greater importance in London – the war in the Middle East.[10]

The Government of India was told to concern itself with the traditional defence of the North-West Frontier, and its army expansion programme, because India had become vital to the prosecution of the imperial war effort in the Middle East, and no distractions from that role – like the defence of Burma against Japan – were tolerable. Immediately after the Fourth Indian division went overseas in August-September 1939, the Indian Army had begun to expand. The 1922-23 reorganization had provided for the doubling of the army in an emergency, but to do this without the loss of quality in a country where the recruits were almost without exception semi-literate peasants required time, especially since the army was simultaneously growing in size and acquiring more sophisticated weapons and equipment. Between the outbreak of the war and May 1940, the Indian Army grew by nearly a third, and a second division was preparing for the Middle East. The second half of 1940, however, saw an expansion that would dwarf what had gone before – and that would have seemed inconceivable in 1939. The 1940 expansion programme called for five infantry divisions (to which a sixth was subsequently added) and an armoured division. Before that programme was complete, the 1941 programme had begun, aimed at four more infantry divisions and another armoured division. When war with Japan broke out the 1942 programme, another four infantry divisions and a third armoured division, was getting under way. The 183,000-man professional army of 1939 had swollen to over a million men, the Royal Indian Navy had grown eightfold, and the Indian Air Force was also expanding rapidly. In addition to fighting formations, India was raising large numbers of labour, base, and lines of communication units as well. In the face of severe shortages of everything except volunteers, this expansion must rank as one of the most impressive achievements of the Government of India and its army, but the immense effort was not without its cost. The dilution of quality was severe, and the huge army being formed in India was being trained exclusively for the Middle East. The Indian Army had been dependent for seventy-five years on recruits from the 'martial classes' drawn predominantly from the Muslim and Sikh population of the Punjab and the North-West Frontier Province. The demands of the expanding army, navy, and air force rapidly exceeded the supply of volunteers from the martial classes, however, and the Indian Army began to take in recruits, particularly for its technical and administrative units, from groups that had not been considered proper military material for a very long time – principally Madrassis. This increased the problems of absorption and training, which were further complicated by the shortage of officers. Pre-war Indian Army officers often had a family connection with India, and sometimes with their regiments, that went back several generations. They knew their men's language and customs and very often the villages from which they came and from which perhaps their fathers and grandfathers had come to serve in the same regiment. This unique characteristic was a source of great strength – and was bound to suffer severely under the pressures of massive expansion. By the autumn of 1941, with the monthly intake running at 50,000 and the army's strength climbing towards the one million mark, the officer shortage had become critical. In June 1940, military service for European British subjects in India had become compulsory and 4,600 men were called up under it to serve as officers while others were sent out from the United Kingdom; but in September 1941 there was a deficiency of 6,500 British officers, and many of those who had joined during the 1940-41 expansion had not had the time to acquire both general professional competence and the special skills that were necessary to lead Indian troops effectively. Nothing shows the desperate urgency with which the Indian Army was being expanded more clearly than the rate at which Indians were receiving the King's commission. 'Indianization' of the army's officer corps had begun shortly after the First World War, but it made very slow progress, and by 1939, there were only some 1,000 Indian officers, about 20 percent of the total. By midsummer 1941, Indians were being commissioned at an annual rate of 900; by early 1942, it would rise to 2,000. The shortage of commissioned officers was compounded by an equal dearth of good quality 'VCOs' – Viceroy's Commissioned Officers, the unique class of Indian warrant officers vital to the smooth functioning of the Army. Here, too, rapid expansion diluted pre-war regulars and brought forward large numbers who, even if capable, were inadequately trained and seasoned. By the end of 1941, the Indian Army as a whole was considerably less efficient than it had been eighteen months before.[11]

Training this burgeoning force was a major problem because qualified instructors were scarce, and material in very short supply. In September 1941 the Commander-in-Chief, India, General Sir Archibald Wavell, pointed out to the War Cabinet that there was not a single modern aircraft, tank, or armoured car in the entire subcontinent. At that date, against the demands of the 1940 expansion programme alone, India had been allotted only 36 percent of its needs in 25-pounder field guns, 23 percent of its requirements for anti-tank guns, and only 4 percent of the necessary anti-tank rifles. Allotted did not mean shipped, much less in the hands of units – and, of course, by the autumn of 1941, a second expansion programme was under way and a third was being planned. Despite everything, training was pushed ahead, but it was training exclusively for the Middle East and the Western Desert, which meant a degree of mechanization completely inappropriate to Burma or Malaya. When in February 1941 a brigade from the 7th Indian Division (of the 1940 expansion programme) was sent to Burma, not only was it trained for the Middle East, but it continued to train for that destination even after it arrived in Burma.[12]

This appropriately indicates Burma's place in imperial strategy prior to the Japanese attack – it existed in a strategic and administrative no-man's land. Its defence was the responsibility of Far East Command at Singapore, but Brooke-Popham, with far more pressing problems closer at hand, only managed three visits in eighteen months. India was responsible for providing reinforcements, but what little could be spared (one brigade in February and a second in December 1941) were new, incompletely trained units, organized for war in the Middle East. London was responsible for providing equipment, but since neither India nor Malaya got what they needed it is not surprising that Burma was virtually ignored. It was nobody's child. Yet from March 1941 Burma began to play an increasingly important role in Anglo-American relations because it was the sole remaining link between China and its western, and principally American, supporters and suppliers. After the Japanese capture of Canton, China's last port, in October 1938, the only way for supplies to reach that country, except across the long land frontier with Russia, was through Rangoon whence there was a good railroad link via Mandalay with the Chinese frontier at Wanting. From there a rough, single lane, fair-weather track to Kunming and Chungking had been hacked out in the autumn of 1938 by an army of 200,000 labourers. This was the famous Burma Road. No other artery of communication carried so little and yet exerted such a great influence on the strategy of the Second World War.

America's deeply emotional involvement with China would require a book in itself to analyse. The material stake of the United States in China, indeed in the Far East as a whole, was small, but the image of a nation struggling towards modernity and eager for American help in that struggle bulked large in many American minds. Its self-appointed role as China's disinterested guardian had been the principal factor in the widening gap between the United States and Japan, and revulsion at Japanese behaviour in China, coupled perhaps with feelings of guilt that American support had hitherto been largely verbal and diplomatic, gave the provision of material aid and its transportation to China a symbolic value out of all proportion to either the amount that could actually be moved to China or its utility once there. To Generalissimo Chiang Kai Shek, American aid was of great importance not only in his struggle with Japan, but in maintaining the internal balance among his generals and with the Communists. Thus, in Chinese and American eyes alike, the Burma Road assumed an importance that its actual carrying capacity by no means warranted. The Japanese also realized the significance of the road and took advantage of Britain's isolation in the summer of 1940 to press for its closure. In no position to face a third opponent the British closed it for three months from 18 July – when heavy rains would in any case have curtailed traffic. Strengthened by victory in the skies over Britain, Churchill and the War Cabinet decided to risk Japanese anger for American goodwill and reopened the road in October. The Prime Minister then tried, unsuccessfully, to use this essentially symbolic gesture to extract some demonstration of American support for Britain in the Far East, such as the visit of a cruiser squadron to Singapore. From this point on, however, Britain was steadily drawn into the web of Sino-American contacts, whose crucial link was Burma.

In November 1940 the Chinese government presented the British Ambassador, Sir Archibald Clark Kerr, with proposals for closer Sino-British cooperation, which included a request for a £50-75 million loan. Somewhat later they suggested that Britain loan 144 pilots to the Chinese air force. The British, however, only advanced a £10 million credit and upgraded the status of the military attaché at Chungking. Simultaneously, the Chinese were pressing their suit in Washington, with requests for 500-1,000 aircraft and a large loan. The Roosevelt administration could not provide the planes either, but added $100 million to the $60 million made available to China since 1938. At the same time Claire L. Chennault, a former United States Army Air Force captain, who had been in China since 1937 and held the rank of colonel in the Chinese Air Force, persuaded his employers to ask for 500 American-manned heavy and medium bombers, with which he undertook to paralyse Japan. Chennault was an extreme development of the 'victory through air power' school, and was to exercise almost as distorting an influence on strategy in the Far East as the Burma Road itself. His request, like that of the Chinese government for 1,000 aircraft, could not be met, but within a few months two events took place which released a flood of American supplies for Chinese use and allowed the direct American participation in China's war with Japan that both Chennault and Chiang desired.

The first of these events was the passage of the Lend Lease Act on 11 March 1941. China was declared eligible for Lend Lease the day the bill became law, and the President approved an initial appropriation of $45,100,000. An American Lend Lease supervisory staff was quickly established in Rangoon, as well as a Chinese supply mission headed by Chiang's cousin, General Yu Fei-Peng. American supplies began to flood in and pile up, because the carrying capacity of the Burma Road, small as it was on the Chinese side, was further reduced by poor organization, lack of adequate repair facilities, drivers and mechanics, and the widespread corruption of the Nationalist regime. By the autumn of 1941, barely 6,000 tons per month were reaching Kunming, whereas the Americans estimated that with proper management 30,000 ought to be possible. American thoughts were turning toward providing that management by running the whole road themselves.

Simultaneously with the development of Lend Lease aid to China, the United States found a way to provide Chiang with a modern air force. Although neither the bombers nor crews Chennault wanted were available, the idea of an American-manned Chinese air force struck a responsive chord in Washington. It promised maximum impact through technology for a relatively small human investment, always an attractive combination in American military eyes. To keep the whole affair 'private', a front organization, Chinese Defense Supplies, Inc, was set up by officials released from the government for the purpose. Roosevelt, as Commander-in-Chief, also released military pilots to engage with the American Volunteer Group (soon immortalized by Hollywood as the 'Flying Tigers'). Lured by high salaries and promises of substantial bonuses for every Japanese aircraft destroyed, Chennault soon had the men he needed.

Equipment was found by taking 100 P-40 (Tomahawk) fighters from the quota allocated to Britain. The AVG began to arrive in Rangoon in June 1941 and the nearby RAF station at Mingaladon was placed at its disposal for the erection and testing of aircraft, while two other RAF bases upcountry, at Toungoo and Magwe, were turned over completely to the Americans. In August London agreed to allow the AVG to do its operational training in Burma, and by December there were four squadrons of what Wavell described as 'formidable buccaneers' there, flying the best aircraft any of the allies had available in the Far East.

The United States War Department had also inserted itself into the picture after the passage of Lend Lease, with a more elaborate and more orthodox plan than Chennault's. The army's idea was to renovate and energize the numerous but ill-equipped and poorly-led Chinese troops with American supplies and advice, turning them into an effective fighting force. The scheme, evolved in the War Department, called for the equipment and training of thirty Chinese divisions – equivalent in strength to about ten British or American divisions. These divisions would spearhead a counter-offensive that would engage the Japanese army so deeply in China that Japan's drive to the south might be arrested. It seemed to be a more hardheaded proposition than Chennault's – if Chinese realities were left out of account. The most important of these realities was that no Chinese commander, whose division was at once his property, the source of his status, and a makeweight in domestic politics, would be at all keen to see a fully equipped and immensely valuable formation used in such a risky way. The decision to adopt a version of Chennault's air power theory and the thirty division scheme at the same time, without ascertaining whether either was practicable or whether the communications to China would carry the material for either, let alone both, is typical of the improvisatory chaos that marked the Roosevelt administration's approach to war. An American military mission to China, headed by a brigadier-general, was approved in July and began to function in October, while supplies for the thirty division scheme added to the congestion on the Rangoon docks.[13]

Around this nexus of Sino-American contacts, subsidiary Sino-British understandings grew up. Burma was of course of prime importance to the Chinese, and in April-May 1941 a

Chinese military mission visited Malaya and Burma. A tentative understanding was reached that a Chinese division would assist in Burma's defence, if the British could supply it (Chinese divisions had virtually no administrative services). There was a stillborn scheme to prepare air fields in China for up to four squadrons of British bombers, and a much more important understanding that some of the AVG would be available to cover Rangoon. To aid Chinese guerrilla operations, a training centre, under the cover name 'School of Bush Warfare', was established at Maymyo, near Mandalay, to turn out British and Indian cadres for Chinese guerrilla companies. Compared to Lend Lease aid, the AVG, and the thirty division scheme, these British contributions were very slight. Britain's real role in American and Chinese eyes was to defend the Burma Road. But even this subsidiary role the British were ill-prepared to play. The only troops available in Burma in the autumn of 1941, the 1st Burma Division, consisted of two shaky brigades of recently raised Burma Rifles battalions, and one Indian brigade trained only for the Middle East. The division lacked transport, signals, guns, and collective training – everything in fact except the divisional designation. A second Indian brigade, also trained for the Middle East, which arrived on the eve of war, was the sole reserve. In the air the RAF had a single squadron (sixteen aircraft) of obsolete American-built Brewster Buffalo fighters, whereas the air defence of Burma was estimated to require at least 280 aircraft.

The Prime Minister in early November, 1941, sent an 'Action This Day' minute to the Chief of the Air Staff, Air Chief Marshal Sir Charles Portal, urging him to send British pilots to join Chennault's force, to turn it into an International Air Force.[14] Nothing came of the idea since spare pilots and time were both lacking, but the minute is instructive. The gesture was clearly intended for American consumption, an obeisance to the American concern with China. No comparable minute enquiring about the state of Burma's defences (or Malaya's) appears in his memoirs, for the defence of the eastern empire had been left to luck and the presumed American ability to deter Japan over a year before. Yet the stage had already been set for the British role in any coalition war against Japan. Virtually unnoticed by Churchill and the British Chiefs of Staff, American planners had begun to envision a war against Japan in which

China played a key role, as a platform for an air offensive or as the source of an army that would tie down Japanese resources. Which of these would become the dominant American strategy for China was not yet clear. Indeed the fight had not yet been fully joined. But for any American strategy predicating an active Chinese role in the defeat of Japan to succeed, the British had to keep open China's door to the outer world. That door was Burma.

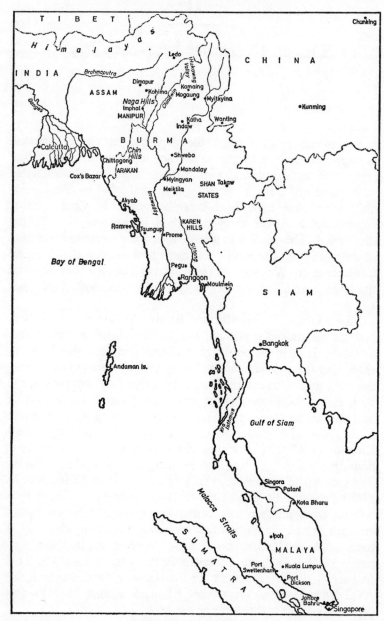

Burma and Malaya.

II

Defeat: December 1941-May 1943

(i)

For eighteen months after the Japanese attack, the British managed the war in Burma to the accompaniment of consistent frustration and disaster, as well as rising American dissatisfaction with presumed British unwillingness, and obvious British inability, to clear their land communications to China, whose importance in American eyes reached its wartime peak during this period. The result was a crisis over the control and direction of the war in the Far East which came to the boil at the 'Trident' Conference in Washington (May 1943) and was not resolved until the next allied summit at Quebec ('Quadrant', September 1943).

Like Malaya, Burma was lost before the first shot was fired. Neither the trained troops nor the aircraft needed to hold it were available. In the six weeks that elapsed between the Japanese entry into the war and the beginning of their invasion of Burma, the only reinforcement that could be scraped up was part of the 17th Indian Division. A 1941 expansion programme division, it had been in existence only a few months, training for the Middle East. Pronounced unfit to face a first class opponent by India's Director of Military Training and promised six weeks intensive divisional training in Iraq before going into action, the division was split up in December, two brigades going to their doom in Malaya and the balance of the division to Burma, followed by a brigade from another new formation to bring it nearly up to strength. Thus, the British had on paper, but in no other way, a force equivalent to the two divisions (each minus its third regiment) of the Japanese Fifteenth Army that crossed the Thai frontier on 20 January 1942. In the air, only the presence of the AVG allowed Rangoon to be defended against the 150-200 Japanese aircraft within striking distance.

The Japanese won the campaign within a month, aided by the inadequacy of the defending forces and by a clumsy British command structure that prevented the best use being made of those that were available. No one had apparently thought it at all anomalous that command in Burma should continue to be treated as an undemanding, end-of-career posting – until Japan attacked. Then Burma was hastily removed from Far East Command and made Wavell's responsibility. On his first visit to Rangoon (21-22 December), he sacked the GOC, Lieutenant-General D. K. McLeod, and replaced him with his own chief of staff, Lieutenant-General Thomas Hutton. Hutton was ordered to hold the Japanese away from Rangoon, the only port through which reinforcements could come. He was thus put in a position very similar to that of Lieutenant-General A. E. Percival in Singapore – a staff officer thrust into a situation that combined command of formations in action on a distant front with heavy administrative responsibilities. Hutton asked for a corps headquarters but did not get one in time. The stage was set for a tense relationship between Hutton and the commander of his principal operational formation, Brigadier (acting Major-General) J. G. Smyth, VC, whose 17th Indian Division stood in the path of the Japanese Fifteenth Army – the 1st Burma Division, gutted of its best troops to bolster Smyth, was left in the Shan States covering another potential invasion route from Thailand. Hutton wanted Smyth to stand as far forward as possible for as long as he could – again there is an echo of Percival's relations with his operational commander, Lieutenant-General Sir Lewis Heath. Smyth, closer to the reality of his own troops' inadequacies and Japanese superiority in numbers and techniques, wanted to fall back to positions where he could fight a concentrated divisional battle behind a river obstacle.[1] The argument between Hutton and Smyth was complicated by the interventions of Wavell, who was by now trying to supervise the defence of Burma not from Delhi, 1,000 miles to the north-west, but from Lembang in Java, an equal distance to the south-east.

This transformation was the result of the first Anglo-American summit meeting of the war – the 'Arcadia' conference in Washington (December 1941-January 1942). At American insistence a theatre command, christened ABDA (American-British-Dutch-Australian), was created to cover the arc from Burma to Australia threatened by the Japanese advance. General George C. Marshall, the US Army's Chief of Staff, who, in the words of one

British observer of the conference, believed that 'unity of command solves all problems', was particularly keen on ABDA.[2] No sooner had the British accepted the idea than they were stunned by American insistence that Wavell should command the new theatre. Liking none of this, the British nonetheless accepted it lest worse befall. The Americans wanted Burma to be part of Wavell's command so that they could bring their weight to bear on decisions involving the defence of their link with China. The British accepted lest Burma be added to the Generalissimo's theatre (Chiang having accepted the position of allied supreme commander in the China theatre, which Roosevelt defined as China, Thailand, and French Indochina). The British Chiefs of Staff thought the American desire to name Wavell supreme commander was a device to shuffle off on the British responsibility for the impending defeats in the Far East. Churchill, however, could hardly refuse to agree to a British supreme commander for a theatre where most of the territory and forces were British or Commonwealth. In any case he wanted American confirmation of the 'Germany first' strategy far more than he wanted to evade American ideas for the conduct of the war against Japan.[3] So Wavell flew off to Java, taking with him responsibility for the defence of Burma, with which he was in only intermittent radio contact, while administrative responsibility and the provision of reinforcements remained with his successor in Delhi, General Sir Alan Hartley. Wavell only managed two hurried visits to Burma (25 January and 5-6 February), amounting to about two days in all, while Hartley never appeared there. Wavell's interventions, which resembled Jovian descents from Olympus, were the reverse of helpful since Wavell, who, rather incredibly, regarded the Japanese as much overrated, felt that a resolute attitude would work wonders. His views had perhaps inordinate weight with Hutton, until recently his chief of staff, and increased the latter's pressure on Smyth to stand on each successive position as long as possible.[4] Wavell's one positive accomplishment was to divert to Rangoon, after his second visit, the 7th Armoured Brigade, which was on its way from the Middle East to Singapore.

Rangoon, and with it Burma, was lost on 20-23 February, a week after Singapore's fall and simultaneously with ABDA's disintegration. Smyth's battered division began to withdraw to the Sittang river, the last major obstacle before Rangoon, on the night of 19/20 February. The retreat was mismanaged through a combination of fatigue, poor communications, excessive mechanization, and a devastating attack by the RAF on the marching columns. A Japanese force reached the bridgehead on the east bank of the Sittang while two-thirds of the 17th Division were still making their way towards it. Then, as a result of a series of errors, Smyth, believing most of his division was safely across, ordered the bridge blown at 5:30 am on 23 February. Although some of the troops on the east bank got back, minus their weapons, the division was temporarily finished as a fighting force. The day after the disaster it mustered some 3,500 men (41 percent of establishment) with about 1,400 rifles and sixty light machine-guns among them.

While this was occurring, further shuffling took place in the British command structure. Neither Wavell nor Churchill and the Chiefs of Staff were happy with the speed of the retreat in Burma, and the Viceroy, Lord Linlithgow, cabled London that Hutton's poor leadership was responsible. On 22 February, Hutton was informed of his impending replacement by General the Hon Sir Harold Alexander, whose chief of staff Hutton was to become. On the same day, communication with Java having virtually ceased, Burma was transferred back to Hartley's command. His responsibility lasted six days until Wavell resumed command in India on the 28th. The previous day, however, Hutton, whose only effective force was now the 7th Armoured Brigade, had decided to evacuate Rangoon, turning back a convoy bringing in another raw Indian brigade. Hartley had agreed with his decision but Wavell immediately countermanded it. On 1 March 1942 he flew up to Burma and, in a remarkable scene on the airfield at Magwe, berated Hutton publicly in front of the Governor, Sir Reginald Dorman-Smith, and the AOC, Air Vice Marshal D. T. Stevenson.[5] Wavell, who in a similar situation a month before had ordered the 18th British Division into Singapore in a vain attempt to prolong its resistance, ordered Rangoon to be held and the convoy carrying the 63rd Indian Infantry Brigade to be turned around a second time. Wavell then visited the 17th Division and ordered that the ailing Smyth be replaced by Brigadier D. T. Cowan (who, ironically, a few months before as Director of Military Training in India had pronounced the division unfit to face a first-class opponent). Three days later Wavell met Alexander briefly at the Calcutta airport and gave him an unequivocal verbal order: 'The retention of Rangoon is a matter of vital importance to our position in the Far East and every effort must be made to hold it.'[6]

Wavell's action nearly destroyed the British forces in Burma. He delayed the evacuation of Rangoon for nearly a week, and as a result of his determination Alexander ordered a counter-attack at Pegu, north-east of Rangoon, almost as soon as he arrived on 5 March. It cost the 63rd brigade its brigadier and all three battalion commanders as well as losses to the armoured brigade and the 17th Division's best remaining brigade. After twenty-four hours, reality prevailed and Alexander ordered the evacuation of the city. By the time it began on the following day, the Japanese had blocked the road to Prome and the north, vital to the withdrawal of the masses of transport characteristic of British and Indian army organization. All attempts to clear the block by the shaken 63rd Brigade failed. Only a lucky chance saved Alexander. The Japanese 33rd Division, unaware that Rangoon was being evacuated, planned to attack from the west. As it swung west across the Prome road it put out a flank guard, which was withdrawn after the divisional column had passed, and Alexander, saved by the good fortune that seems always to have attended him, withdrew north into the Irrawaddy valley, as the Japanese entered the empty, burning capital of Burma.

The remaining three months of the campaign can be dealt with very briefly. Control of Rangoon allowed the Japanese to pour in reinforcements, better than doubling the strength of the Fifteenth Army. Two divisions and two tank regiments arrived in March and early April, while the supporting Fifth Air Division was brought up to 420 aircraft. By contrast, the British force was a wasting asset. No further reinforcements could reach it, and Alexander's two divisions were already badly under strength. On 19 March, 17th Indian Division had a 'rifle strength' of 6,700, somewhat more than half its authorized total, while the only effective units in the 1st Burma Division were three Indian battalions, its Burmese units having been depleted by desertion or dismissal to their homes. In the air the RAF and the AVG, which together had about 150 aircraft in early March, were overwhelmed during the course of the month. Henceforth, the sky belonged to the Japanese. Three things made the long fighting retreat possible. Hutton's foresight, and the abilities of his chief administrative officer, Major-General E. N. Goddard, had allowed the transfer from Rangoon to Mandalay and upper Burma of sufficient supplies and base installations to support the rapidly dwindling British force during its withdrawal. Hutton's request for a corps headquarters was finally met in March, with the arrival from Iraq of Lieutenant-General W. J. Slim to assume command of the hastily improvised 'Burcorps'. Perhaps the finest British general of the war, Slim's leadership in the field ideally complemented Alexander's at Burma Army headquarters. Finally, there was the 7th Armoured Brigade, whose tanks, and fighting skill, provided a hard core which time and again was Burcorps' salvation. Without the armoured brigade's signals, Burcorps would often have been paralysed for lack of communications, so poorly equipped was Slim's headquarters.

Alexander had to conduct the retreat with the handicap of not knowing exactly where he was supposed to retreat to. Between his meeting with Wavell at Calcutta on 4 March and 18 April, he received no further directives from either Delhi or London, nor did his headquarters even have a radio capable of reaching India. On the latter date a letter from Wavell arrived, telling Alexander that, in the event a withdrawal from Burma became necessary, part of his force would fall back into Assam and part would retire into China alongside the Chinese Expeditionary Force that had been fighting in Burma. This order, administratively unsound if politically attractive, was virtually impossible to execute when it was issued and ran into Slim's unswerving determination that none of his troops were going to end their long retreat in famine-stricken Yunnan. On 23 April, six days before the Japanese captured Lashio and cut the Burma Road, Alexander told Wavell that the supply situation made it necessary to withdraw his entire force into Assam, where it arrived, in a dead heat with the monsoon, early in May.[7] Wavell's order of 18 April, however, indicated how important the Chinese factor had become in decisions about Burma.

Prior to the Japanese attack on the United States and British territories, the Chinese had made tentative commitments of a division and part of the AVG for the defence of Burma, which was more important to them than it was to Britain. On 8 Decem-

ber Chiang confirmed the offer of a division to Major-General
L. E. Dennys, the head of the British Military Mission in Chungking. A week later, by which time the dimensions of the initial
Anglo-American disasters were becoming apparent, Chiang
offered Dennys 50,000 men for Burma, and the following day
his Minister of War told Dennys that the Fifth and Sixth Chinese
Armies could be made available. The proviso made when a single
division was being discussed remained, however – the British
authorities in Burma would have to supply, pay, and move the
Chinese troops. Chiang introduced a second precondition in his
conversation with Dennys on the 15th. The Chinese, he said,
must be given a separate operational area and line of communications and not combined with British forces in any way. It was
against this background that Wavell arrived in Chungking on
22 December, accompanied by Major-General G. H. Brett of
the United States Army Air Force, for a hastily-arranged inter-
allied conference. The idea for the meeting had originated with
Roosevelt, but the British fell in with it readily enough, because
closer liaison with the Chinese seemed to offer considerable
advantages. On 23-24 December, a series of conversations at
cross purposes took place between Chiang and Wavell, with Brett
and the head of the American Military Mission, Brigadier-
General John Magruder, in attendance. Chiang wanted to talk
about global strategy; Wavell wanted to secure as much of the
AVG as possible to augment Burma's air defences, as well as
some of the Chinese Lend Lease supplies piled up in Rangoon
to make good Burma Army's manifold deficiencies. The real
crux of the discussion, however, was the Chinese offer of two
armies. Chiang made it clear he wanted them committed *en
masse* to minimize chances of a setback with its resulting loss of
face. Wavell, however, stuck to the pre-war arrangement, accepting only one division of the Sixth Army and asking that a second
be moved up to the frontier in reserve. Chiang was deeply
offended, and Anglo-Chinese wartime cooperation got off to a
very bad start, for which Wavell was sharply criticized then and
later. This was not entirely fair to Wavell, for the Chinese were
certainly offering less than appeared. The fighting strength of two
armies (six divisions) was about that of two British divisions, and
they had little in the way of supporting arms and almost no
administrative services. In some units not even all the infantry

had rifles. The British would not only have to improvise arrangements for their supply, but pay and move them as well as allow them to operate independently of British command. Yet the organizational weaknesses of the Chinese and the command problems their presence in Burma would pose were not the principal factors in Wavell's decision, as he candidly admitted in his Despatch six years later. He felt, he wrote then, that 'it was desirable that a country of the British Empire should be defended by Imperial troops rather than by foreign.' It was not yet apparent to Wavell that Singapore would fall, and Burma had not yet been seriously attacked. Wavell claimed that he felt he would have enough Imperial troops to hold Burma, although by the time he met Chiang half the forces promised him by the Chiefs of Staff ten days earlier had already been nibbled away to bolster the crumbling defences of Malaya. Wavell, who did not take the Japanese seriously enough, evidently found it hard to accept that 'a country of the British Empire' needed Chinese assistance in its defence.[8] Once the Japanese invasion of Burma began in earnest, Hutton quickly asked Wavell to lift his ban on the entry of further Chinese troops. By early February the move of the Sixth Army into the Shan States and the concentration of the Fifth at Toungoo in the Sittang Valley had been agreed, and, after the fall of Rangoon, the Sixty-Sixth Chinese Army moved into Burma as well. Although it is doubtful whether Wavell's reluctance to accept more Chinese earlier made much difference to the defence of Rangoon, in the second stage of the campaign the Chinese forces, roughly equivalent in size to the British, occupied the attention of three of the Japanese Fifteenth Army's four divisions, perhaps saving Burcorps from complete destruction.

The effect of Wavell's action was seen most strikingly, not in the field but at the summit of Anglo-American relations. Churchill reported from Washington to the War Cabinet that Wavell's attitude at the Chungking conference had made a very poor impression.[9] This was worsened by disputes over the use and disposition of the Chinese Lend Lease supplies in Rangoon. Indeed his stay in Washington made Churchill fully aware, for the first time, of the value placed on China in the United States. Nine years later he wrote about 'what I felt was a wholly unreal standard of values,' which 'accorded China almost an equal fighting power with the British Empire, and rated the Chinese armies as a factor to be mentioned in the same breath as the armies of Russia.'[10] However perverse this struck him, it was a political fact the Prime Minister could not ignore. It affected his decision on the establishment of ABDA, and the inclusion of Burma in it, over the protests of the Governor. When he returned to England the new orientation of his thoughts was quickly shown. Conscious that Marshall, on 10 January, had proposed that the operation *and defence* of the Burma Road should be handed over to the United States, Churchill sent a minute to his personal chief of staff, Lieutenant-General Sir Hastings Ismay, on 21 January for consideration by the Chiefs of Staff, in which he asked whether 'we should not at once blow the docks and batteries and workshops [at Singapore] to pieces and concentrate everything on the defence of Burma and the Burma Road.'[11] Two days later he cabled Wavell a succinct summary of his experiences in Washington: 'If I can epitomise in one word the lesson I learned in the United States, it was "China." '[12] As important politically as China was, however, the burden of Singapore was inescapable. The Australian government reacted very sharply to reports of Churchill's proposal reaching them from Sir Earle Page, their special representative in London. Politics more than strategy dictated the subsequent decision to allow the two brigades of the 18th Division still at sea to continue on to Singapore. Churchill did not, however, lose sight of Burma. The day after Singapore fell, he signalled to Dorman-Smith that he regarded the maintenance of contact with China via Burma as the most important feature of the war in the East,[13] and he immediately plunged into telegraphic battle with the Australian government to secure their 7th Division, returning from the Middle East, for Burma. Despite intense pressure from the Prime Minister, seconded by Roosevelt, the Australians adamantly insisted on the return of the division, and the 6th following it. Since the 7th Division was not tactically loaded and could only have reached Rangoon piecemeal between 26 February and 6 March, Australian stubbornness may have saved Churchill from a second Singapore. The failure to find enough 'imperial forces' to hold Rangoon, however, made the British reluctance to accept Chinese assistance more culpable in American eyes and made it impossible to prevent the establishment of an American theatre command in South-East Asia.

One of the fruits of the Arcadia Conference was an offer to Chiang of the supreme command of all allied forces in the China theatre. When the Generalissimo accepted this empty honour, he shrewdly asked for an American as his chief of staff in his new capacity. Thus, a senior American officer was inserted into the command arrangements in the Far East to watch over the single, dominating American interest in the area – contact with China via Burma. Lieutenant-General Joseph W. Stilwell, who had served in China in the thirties, knew the language, and, after his fashion, liked the people, became Chiang's chief of staff. He added to this a number of other appointments, making him virtually the American plenipotentiary in South-East Asia: Lend Lease administrator, member designate of any allied war council in the area, and, most important of all, commander of the new American CBI (China-Burma-India) theatre. The last appointment was crucial. Stilwell was to control not only any American forces sent to China or South-East Asia, but a base area in India that would support their operations and the trans-Himalayan air lift that would soon take the place of the defunct Burma Road. After the dissolution of ABDA – which occurred before he actually reached Burma – Stilwell was not responsible to any of the British authorities in the area, the Viceroy or the Commander-in-Chief, India, much less to the British Chiefs of Staff. Reporting as he did to the Joint Chiefs of Staff in Washington, Stilwell was a nearly independent war-lord, a position reinforced by his prickly, acerbic nature and his deep suspicion of the determination and ability of the 'limeys', an attitude that his arrival at a low point in British military fortunes did nothing to change. Marshall later claimed that American domestic politics made necessary the pretence that all American personnel and material in South-East Asia were there to support China. That the political imperative was real is not in question. It is much harder to see that there was any pretence about it. Stilwell's position is the best evidence in this respect, especially when contrasted with the command arrangements later made in Europe, where a different set of political considerations ruled. The American interest in South-East Asia was a link with China, *tout court*. By retaining control of all American resources there in the hands of American commanders directly responsible to Washington, the utilization of those resources solely to further

American policy was assured. Only if this is understood does CBI and its later permutations make sense. Although never openly acknowledged as such, Stilwell's anomalous position was an anti-British move. Roosevelt and Marshall knew the British did not share either the American hope for effective Chinese participation in the war or the President's vision of China as one of the postwar great powers, and they knew they could not expect the British to place aid to China on the same level of importance as they did. The Americans, therefore, took steps to see that their policy could be pursued independently of the British authorities who controlled their Indian base. The security of that base, together with a traditional suspicion of British imperialism, led as well to Roosevelt's tentative probes, encouraged by Chiang, in February and March into relations between Britain and the Congress Party in India, which were deteriorating as the prestige of the Raj was eroded by military defeat. At the outset, Anglo-American cooperation in South-East Asia was flawed by a basic difference about the object of the war there.

All this made little difference at first. Stilwell did not even reach Burma until after the fall of Rangoon. The Chinese army did not operate according to western principles of military organization, and although Chiang told Stilwell that he was in 'command' of all the Chinese forces in Burma, he never entrusted Stilwell with the seal that would have given some reality to the position. Chiang also gave Alexander 'command' of the three Chinese armies at a conference in Chungking on 24 March. Neither Alexander nor Stilwell actually exercised anything more than paper authority over the Chinese – Stilwell on one occasion was reduced to offering a 50,000 rupee bribe to one of his divisional commanders to procure an attack – which is probably what Chiang always intended, and perhaps all he could really give. In spite of their contrasting personalities, Stilwell's anomalous position, and an atmosphere of chaos and defeat, cooperation between Stilwell, Alexander and Slim was relatively good. But the end of the campaign, with Stilwell and the best part of two divisions of the Sixty-Sixth Army trudging over the hills into Assam, left everyone's preconceptions intact. The Chinese had made a poor impression on the British – or, rather, confirmed the low opinion they already held, while Stilwell was convinced that British and Indian military ability and will were alike wanting, but that with a rebuilt Chinese army, he could reopen the Burma Road.

(ii)

Churchill minuted to the Chiefs of Staff on 4 April 1942 that he wanted plans framed for 'a counter-offensive on the Eastern front in the summer or autumn.'[14] Twelve days later, as Slim withdrew Burcorps through the blazing oilfields at Yenangyaung in 114 degree heat, Wavell sent a note to his Chief of Staff, Lieutenant-General E. L. Morris: 'I want the [Indian] Joint Planning Staff to begin as soon as possible consideration of an offensive to reoccupy Burma.'[15] These two minutes, initiating the planning for a counter-offensive against Japan, were, however, quickly overshadowed by a threat that the Prime Minister and Chiefs of Staff considered more immediate and far more urgent. The Japanese naval raid into the Bay of Bengal and the carrier attacks on Ceylon during Eastertide (5-9 April) seemed to portend loss of maritime control in the Indian Ocean, which would have had devastating consequences for the British position in the Middle East. For the next six weeks London concentrated on securing its hold on the western Indian Ocean and communications with Egypt and the Persian Gulf. The preemptive seizure of Madagascar, mooted as far back as December 1940, absorbed more and more of the reinforcements, assault shipping, and landing craft promised to Wavell, despite a stark warning, set in boldface type, presented to the Chiefs of Staff by their Joint Planners at the beginning of April: 'we are in real danger of losing our Indian Empire.'[16] At the end of that month the custodians of that Empire, Wavell and Linlithgow, cabled angrily to Churchill: 'The War Cabinet must really make up their minds whether or not they propose to defend India and Ceylon seriously.'[17] In vain they asked the Prime Minister to put their cable before the full War Cabinet. Yet no sooner had the success of the Madagascar operations released some assault shipping and troops, than the decision to mount 'Torch', the crisis in the desert war against Rommel, and the need to succour beleaguered Malta, deprived Wavell of them again. Against this discouraging background, planning for offensive operations against Japan had a considerable degree of unreality about it.

The Chiefs of Staff replied to Churchill's 4 April minute a

month later. They pointed out that the most useful offensive operation in the east would be an amphibious assault on Rangoon, but that since this would require naval superiority in the Bay of Bengal, air superiority over southern Burma, the necessary assault shipping and landing craft, and enough properly trained troops for both the assault and follow-up, nothing of value was feasible for the time being.[18] Six days later India's Joint Planning Staff produced its assessment of the problem Wavell had set. They began by posing a very pertinent question: what was the object of operations based on India? If it was merely the reconquest of northern Burma to reopen communications with China, this could be obtained by an overland attack from Assam, although the maintenance of the position, with the Japanese in control of Rangoon, would be precarious. If, however, the reconquest of Burma by recapturing Rangoon was the aim, overland operations were relatively unimportant. Control of the Bay of Bengal, air superiority, and the preliminary seizure of airfield sites on the Arakan coast were the requisites – and, once these were available, a much more ambitious strategy came into view. Rangoon could be bypassed in favour of Moulmein, from which a threat could be mounted against Bangkok and Japanese shipping in the Gulf of Siam.[19] To sketch such a strategy, and its attendant requirements, was to indicate its impossibility in May 1942. But this paper raised the question of the object for which the British were fighting in the east, a question which was never properly to be answered. It also sketched out the two contending strategies for India-based operations around which subsequent argument would swirl – the overland versus the maritime or amphibious. The latter clearly offered greater opportunities of damaging Japan, but it required resources that were not in sight – and would do nothing to restore communications with China.

Churchill and the Chiefs of Staff clearly preferred the amphibious strategy. On 18 May the Prime Minister again minuted about the desirability of an autumn offensive 'from Moulmein to Assam' and at the end of the month cabled Wavell that Rangoon by the end of September ought to be his aim. When Wavell replied that only a limited operation to clear part of north Burma might be possible during the 1942-43 dry season (October-May), Churchill brushed this aside, as 'nice and useful nibbling' and called again for a series of operations to take Akyab on the

Arakan coast, followed by amphibious descents on Rangoon and Moulmein, with Bangkok as the ultimate objective.[20] This may have been what Michael Howard has called it, 'cigar butt strategy', or it may have been no more than the usual Churchillian prodding to encourage imaginativeness and an offensive attitude in a commander, although Wavell was never lacking in either. Alexander, returning to London after the dissolution of Burma Army headquarters, was given the task of reporting Wavell's full plan for the reconquest of Burma to Churchill and the Chiefs of Staff, perhaps in the hope of making the impossibility of any major operations plain to the Prime Minister. Wavell's plan called for a diversion to pin down Japanese strength in north Burma, followed by the seizure of airfields at two sites on the Arakan coast and then a two-division assault on Rangoon. The outline plan was accompanied by a lengthy catalogue of India Command's needs, and a request for American action to divert Japanese air and naval strength to the Pacific while British operations were in progress.

Alexander placed all this before the Chiefs of Staff on 10 July and by the 12th the Prime Minister had been convinced that an ambitious 'general offensive' was not possible in the autumn of 1942. Wavell's plan became the framework for operation 'Anakim', and planning and preparations were ordered on the assumption that it would take place before the 1943 monsoon broke the following May. Churchill, however, laid down that it would be dependent on the course of events in Europe and the Middle East, as well as on a substantial reduction in Japanese air strength in Burma. He added that the Australian and American activities in the Pacific would have to engage the Japanese closely enough to prevent them reinforcing Burma before and during 'Anakim'.[21] By mid-July 1942 Churchill had convinced himself that nothing substantial could be done in the east for the balance of the year, and had established the basis for a British amphibious strategy, aimed ultimately at Bangkok, in 1943 – circumstances permitting. General Marshall, Admiral Ernest King (the United States' Chief of Naval Operations) and Harry Hopkins, Roosevelt's closest confidant, were on their way to London for the climactic discussions on the proposed North African operation which had been Churchill's first priority since American entry into the war. The Prime Minister was well content to leave matters in the east – not until the Casablanca conference would he again seriously concern himself with Burma. 'Anakim', however, brought no immediate prospect of reopening the road to China, and, therefore, offered nothing to the Americans, Chiang, or Stilwell, and in July the latter produced his own blueprint for clearing Burma.

By midsummer 1942, there was a very elaborate American command structure in India. Stilwell's CBI headquarters were now in Delhi, although Stilwell himself was often in Chungking. Delhi was also the headquarters of the 10th United States Air Force, and the India-China Ferry Command, responsible for the airlift over the Himalayas that had replaced the Burma Road as the link with China. A supply organization based on Karachi supported all three. In China itself, fed by the 'Hump' airlift, the AVG, formally reincorporated into the Army Air Force on 4 July 1942 and renamed the China Air Task Force, remained under Chennault's command but subordinate to the 10th Air Force in Delhi. There was little internal unity within the American camp. Stilwell controlled the 10th Air Force, but its commander (Brigadier-General Clayton Bissell) and Chennault, once again on active duty and recently promoted to brigadier-general, intensely disliked one another, as did Stilwell and Chennault. The American organizations were completely independent of the British authorities in India, who, in any case, had enough on their hands without worrying overly about what the Americans might be planning. Nevertheless, it says a great deal for Stilwell's determination that within two months of his arrival in India he had a plan for the restoration of communications with China by the reconquest of north Burma, based on three elements: the airlift, the Chinese troops who had retired from Burma into Assam, and the Ledo Road.

The Hump airlift, the expansion of the RAF in India to its target figure of sixty-six squadrons, plus the requirements of the 10th Air Force had necessitated an increase in the number of airfields in India Command to 215 (in March 1942 there were only 16 all-weather fields in India and Ceylon) – an enormous undertaking in a country where engineering resources and skilled labour were scarce, and the internal transportation system already strained to the breaking point. Nevertheless, CBI planners assumed that the airlift tonnage would not only support Chennault but allow the thirty-division plan to proceed, although at a slower rate. The two divisions of the Chinese Sixty-Sixth Army, which had retired to India, had been regrouped at Ramgarh in Assam, where India Command fed and housed them, while the Americans provided equipment and instructors. Stilwell was convinced that, removed from the pernicious atmosphere of Chinese politics and the corrupt chaos that passed for Chinese military administration, he could turn them into a first-class fighting force, capable of spearheading a drive from his railhead at Ledo in Assam, down the Hukawng Valley into north Burma, covering the construction of an all-weather road. The plan, combining all these elements, that Stilwell put forward in July, called for a concentric attack on north Burma (at that time garrisoned by one Japanese division) in March 1943 by a force of twelve American-equipped Chinese divisions from Yunnan, his own two Chinese divisions from Ledo, and three British divisions from Assam. The object would be the clearance of enough territory to drive a road from Ledo through to connect up with the old Burma Road, meanwhile securing airbases that would allow the airlift to follow an easier route and to enjoy fighter protection throughout.[22] Stilwell's plan was limited to reopening a road to China and had no amphibious component, although he realized that China's supply problems could only be finally solved by reopening Rangoon, which he planned to do ultimately by an advance overland from the north. But on 1 August his nominal superior weighed in with demands that were more compatible with 'Anakim' than with Stilwell's proposals.

Chiang, who in late June had demanded a fifty-fold increase in the airlift by August, plus a first line strength of 500 aircraft for Chennault (who then had sixty-four) and three American divisions, now insisted that before any Chinese forces could take part in an attack on Burma, the British would have to assert naval control of the Bay of Bengal and mount operations against the Andaman Islands and Rangoon.[23] This would certainly have guaranteed the success of any attack on north Burma, but it would also have made it unnecessary by opening the way for the British to follow their own preferred amphibious strategy. It is doubtful whether Chiang ever realized this. In any case, Churchill and the Chiefs of Staff had ruled out anything amphibious in the Bay of Bengal a fortnight earlier, and events in India and on the north-east frontier were reducing the chances of British offensive activity even further.

The troops which Wavell finally got after the operations in Madagascar were riddled with malaria and required prolonged convalescence. More seriously, the declining prestige of the Raj tempted the Congress leaders to make a bid, summarized in Gandhi's 'Quit India' slogan, to attain immediately their political aims. Rejecting the War Cabinet's offer, conveyed by the Cripps Mission, of dominion status after the war (an offer which had the incidental effect of removing the maintenance of British power in the east as the object of British strategy there, without making clear what, besides victory over Japan, was the War Cabinet's aim), Congress moved rapidly toward a breach with the government, which occurred with the arrest of the Congress leaders on 9 August and the outbreak two days later of the widespread disturbances, in Madras, Bihar and the United Provinces, known as the 'Congress Revolt'. Although quickly contained, Wavell was forced to use fifty-seven battalions on internal security duties including thirty-one (the infantry strength of three divisions) drawn from either his field army or troops in training for it. Finally, the 1942 monsoon was exceptionally heavy, making even the maintenance of IV Corps in Assam precarious, while malaria simultaneously decimated the troops there, the sick rate reaching 40 percent. On 15 September, Wavell warned the Chiefs of Staff that a limited offensive to take Akyab, raids into north Burma, and the improvement of communications to the north-east frontier were the maximum he could hope for during the 1942-43 dry season.[24] Two days later he sent his Chief of Staff a paper, 'Operation Fantastical', which illustrates both his great strengths and considerable weaknesses as the manager of the British war effort in the east. 'We have got a difficult problem from an orthodox point of view and we shall never solve it by purely orthodox thinking and orthodox methods,' he wrote. 'We should still be holding Burma ourselves if the Japanese had thought and acted on purely orthodox lines.' Then he went on to pose some farsighted questions: 'To what extent can we live on the country? How far can we meet our transport requirements by unorthodox methods . . . Is it really impossible to operate in Burma in the rainy season?' But Wavell still clung obstinately to the belief that the Japanese were not as formidable as everyone thought: 'We may find Japanese opposition very much lower than we expect in Burma if we can only act with boldness and determination . . . The Jap has never fought defensively and may not be much good at it.'[25] Disaster lurked in this last assumption. Wavell's insight, imagination, and long-range vision often faltered in contact with immediate tactical problems. He had shown this once before in Burma. He was about to show it again.

Another area where Wavell's touch was less than sure was his relations with Stilwell. Some of this was the fault of a command structure that allowed two independent commands, planning quite different strategies, to exist side by side, linked only at the distant summit in Washington. Wavell and Stilwell both had their headquarters in Delhi, but Wavell, in addition to his immense responsibilities for the conduct of operations and the administration of the Indian Army, had great political responsibilities as a member of the Government of India at a time of crisis, while Stilwell was often in Ramgarh or Chungking. Nor is it likely that the reserved, taciturn Wavell failed to arouse Stilwell's simmering anglophobia. Only some such conjunction of faulty arrangements and discordant personalities can explain the confusion that began to develop in October.

Chiang finally approved Stilwell's July plan on 14 October but maintained his insistence on a force of three or four battleships and six to eight carriers to dominate not only the Bay of Bengal, but the Java and China Seas as well, plus the capture of Rangoon. The British obviously could not meet these demands, but Roosevelt promised to increase Chennault's force to 500 aircraft, raise the number of ferry aircraft on the Hump route, and double the number of Chinese divisions to be reequipped. Chiang thus got American agreement to most of his June demands, and the way seemed clear for Stilwell to press ahead. He met Wavell in Delhi on 17 October to thrash out plans for the upcoming dry season. Stilwell's proposal fitted in closely enough with 'Anakim' for the two to be glued together, although the objects of the two operations had almost nothing in common – and, in any case, Wavell had known for a month that 'Anakim' was not very likely. Wavell met Stilwell again on the 27th to discuss further the arrangements for the combined attack on Burma, but the day before he had again warned the Chiefs of Staff that 'Anakim' was not possible before the 1943 monsoon, and on 20 November he received a new target date for the operation – 1 October 1943. The reconquest of Burma had now been officially put back to the 1943-44 dry season. Not until 12 December, however, did Wavell pass this on to Stilwell.[26] For three months after he knew 'Anakim' was clearly out of the question before the 1943 monsoon, Wavell had been shadowboxing with Stilwell. It is true that he still planned limited operations in north Burma, and that in any case Chiang had reneged again shortly after the Delhi conferences, refusing to move unless the British assured him of naval superiority in the Bay of Bengal and air superiority over Burma, but Stilwell's exasperated diary entry early in January, 1943 – 'the Limeys . . . will quit, the Chinese will quit, and the god-damned Americans can go ahead and fight' – reflects an understandable feeling of betrayal that would soon have its repercussions at the summit.[27]

From 'Arcadia' to Casablanca, affairs in the Far East were overshadowed for the British by the war in the west. In the redivision of global strategic responsibility between Great Britain and the United States which took place in the spring of 1942 after the collapse of ABDA, South and South-East Asia became recognized areas of British responsibility, and thereafter the Americans received little information about what the British planned to do there, and Stilwell received nothing at all from Wavell (who feared it might leak to the Japanese via Chungking) until the misleading conference at Delhi in October. There was little connection between the nearly separate wars the two allies waged against Japan. When Churchill appealed in April for a naval diversion in the Pacific to take the pressure off the Indian Ocean, there was little the Americans could do. Nor could the British respond to American requests for action by the virtually nonexistent Eastern Fleet before the battle of Midway (3-6 June), and again as United States forces struggled for a foothold on Guadalcanal in August and September. China remained the only point of contact. At a meeting of the largely decorative Pacific War Council in May, the Chinese claimed that Churchill had promised that the British would provide a fleet capable of reestablishing control of the Bay of Bengal. The minutes of the meeting do not support this, but the Prime Minister, who knew the importance of China in American eyes, and whose cables to Wavell reveal his hope of rebuilding the Eastern Fleet over the summer, may have made encouraging noises that Chiang was later to use with considerable effect.[28] Nevertheless, offensive action in Europe or North Africa was the staple of Anglo-American exchanges over the summer. At the Washington conference in June, Brooke dismissed operations in Burma with the observation that an offensive there to reopen communications with China was pointless divorced from a concerted allied offensive against Japan.[29] Yet throughout this period American concern that China might collapse was mounting and with it anxiety to bring some speedy relief to Chiang. The British Chiefs of Staff were less impressed by what China could contribute to the war, and more sceptical of the benefit likely to be derived from the immense effort required to get material to China. Their opinion was reinforced by the observations of Major-General G. E. Grimsdale, who had succeeded Dennys (killed in an air crash) as head of the British Military Mission, and who reported that the Chinese made very little use of the supplies they received.[30] Furthermore, British authorities generally at this stage of the war resented American intrusion into the question of operations based on India, a sphere that they regarded as exclusively their concern. Field-Marshal Sir John Dill, the head of the British Staff Mission in Washington, had tactfully to remind Brooke in September that consideration for American views on China was the price the British would have to pay for imposing their views on alliance strategic policy in the west. Marshall, Dill reported, believed that the Americans could handle the Chinese better than the British, which was probably true enough, given the British reluctance to handle them at all.[31] Wavell's apparently forthcoming attitude with Stilwell in October, after nearly eight months of non-communication, probably owed as much to his recognition, encouraged by Dill, of its value to Anglo-American amity as to any belief in the workability of the plans Stilwell was proposing.

Into this tangle of cross-purposes and conflicting strategies, another element was introduced by Chennault's insistence that air power alone could sustain China. In July he promised that given one hundred modern fighters and thirty bombers, he could cripple Japanese activity in China, thus resurrecting the claim he had first made in the autumn of 1940. If adopted, his strategy would have required little military effort by the Chinese forces, and would have undercut the War Department's dream of a great modernized Chinese army. Chennault's plan would also require an airlift of 2,000 tons a month (roughly four times what the Hump route was actually delivering in the autumn of 1942), thus negating the possibility of the War Department scheme in another way. Chennault had Chiang's ear in a way that Stilwell never did, as the Generalissimo's demands for more aircraft and airlift tonnage showed, and the 'air power strategy' soon gained the support of Roosevelt and Hopkins. The promise of more aircraft for both the China Air Task Force and the Hump was a barometer of Chennault's success, although the President characteristically indicated continued support for the War Department by agreeing at the same time to double the thirty division programme.[32] As the autumn of 1942 turned to winter, there were two competing American strategies for the support of China (with the President generously sustaining both), a conflicting British amphibious strategy whose framers lacked the resources to execute it, and the intractable reality of Burma. Out of this morass the British and American planners and their political masters now tried to shape a coherent strategy.

Even before 'Torch' was launched, the Chiefs of Staff approved a 'Strategic Review' looking forward to the operations that would become possible in 1943. The emphasis, as always, was on the European theatre. In the war against Japan they suggested that the 'liquidation' of China should be prevented, and the specifically British contribution to this should be operations in Burma to reopen a land route into China. They added, however, that nothing done in the east could be allowed to interfere with the development of the war against Germany, and that any operations in Burma would be dependent on the availability of forces.[33] Ten days before they approved this paper, the Chiefs of Staff had given Wavell a target date for 'Anakim' of 1 October 1943. The review was unexceptionable on the premise, perfectly valid in London, that the war against Germany was the one that counted, but would have confirmed Stilwell's worse fears had he seen it, as would developments over the next two months in London. The War Office produced a paper on the reconquest of Burma in November that declared Chinese cooperation unlikely to materialize, or to be very·valuable if it did, since American aid was unlikely to remedy the fundamental defects of the Nationalist armies. The War Office was also clear that control of all planning and operations must be centralized in Wavell.[34] The War Cabinet had already shown itself nervous about the ambiguous position of the Chinese at Ramgarh, a reaction to Chiang's flirtation with Gandhi some months before. On his sixty-eighth birthday, Churchill, at a Chiefs of Staff meeting, ruled that it was not necessary to tell Chiang about the changes in the plans for 'Anakim' – a course of action Wavell had been following toward the Generalissimo and his American chief of staff for some time.[35] When the American Joint Chiefs of Staff forwarded to London a plan of their own for the clearance of north Burma, the Chiefs of Staff told Wavell to warn Stilwell that nothing must be undertaken in north Burma that would in any way prejudice an autumn 'Anakim'.[36] Wavell, who had already let it be known that he doubted the feasibility even of limited operations in north Burma during the spring of 1943, administered this additional cold douche to the harassed CBI commander on 20 December.[37] On New Year's Eve, the Chiefs of Staff approved a paper that summarized the British approach to the forthcoming 'Symbol' conference at Casablanca. In its fifty-two paragraphs, Burma rated two sentences: 'The only way of bringing material help to China is to open the Burma Road. The reconquest of Burma should therefore be undertaken as soon as resources permit.'[38] The main theme of the British paper was a reaffirmation of 'Germany first'. At 'Arcadia', America was new to the war, and the American service chiefs ill-prepared and preoccupied. At Casablanca the first real clash over alliance strategy took place.

The arguments at Casablanca about operations in Burma took place against a background of Anglo-American disagreement over strategy in Europe, which served to sharpen American distrust of British ideas about the war in Asia. The British quickly discovered, with a sense of shock, that the Americans regarded the Pacific as their affair about which Britain would be informed, but not consulted.[39] Since there was no British contribution to the Pacific war, and since even information had been scanty about British plans for Burma, the surprise is rather hard to understand, except on the basis of a British feeling that in wisdom, practical experience of war, and forces engaged, they were the senior partners in the alliance, an understandable but already obsolete idea. The British also discovered that some doubts were entertained about their willingness to contribute to the defeat of Japan after victory over Germany[40], doubts fed by apparent British lukewarmness over aiding China by reconquering Burma, an operation which had become for the Americans a touchstone of British good faith in the war against Japan.

Chiang had sent two telegrams to the President shortly before the conference began, complaining about Churchill's broken 'promise' to put a fleet into the Bay of Bengal.[41] Churchill, to whom Roosevelt forwarded Chiang's cables, was always alert for potential snags in Anglo-American cooperation, and quickly realized the importance of meeting the Americans over Burma. He had in any case been from the beginning a keen supporter of an amphibious strategy of reconquest in South-East Asia. On 15 January, at a meeting with the British Chiefs of Staff, he made it clear that *his* programme for 1943 included the reconquest of Burma.[42] Some months later he confirmed the essentially political nature of his decision, remarking to the War Cabinet that 'at Casablanca we had agreed – largely as a concession to United States opinion – to mount a full scale operation for the recapture of Burma between the monsoons of 1943 and 1944.'[43] The political decision to placate the Americans about Burma once taken, agreement on strategy followed quickly. At a Combined Chiefs of Staff meeting on the 18th, the United States Joint Chiefs offered to make up British deficiencies in landing craft and naval support for an autumn 'Anakim', and the agreement to mount the operation was included in the paper on the 'Conduct of the War in 1943' approved by the Combined Chiefs the following day, although it still remained subject both to final confirmation in the summer, and to the European situation. Over the next four days, however, the President's intervention (and the impact of Chennault's ideas on him) produced a more complex and muddled plan in the final report presented by the Combined Chiefs to their political superiors. 'Anakim' remained, but two new operations were added: a limited offensive in north Burma to protect and improve the air transport route to China, and an increased tempo of operations by Chennault's air force in China itself.[44] The British Joint Planning Staff pointed out the fallacy in Roosevelt's approach, noting that 'the Burma Road cannot be opened to give effective assistance to the Chinese until virtually the whole of Burma has been reconquered. This operation ('Anakim') cannot be undertaken before the monsoon of 1943, and may not be possible until after the defeat of Germany.'[45] The clear implication was that preliminary operations in north Burma consumed resources to no very great advantage. But the President and the Prime Minister had both accomplished their essentially political objects. Chennault's (and Chiang's) air power strategy had received partial endorsement, and a programme of activity in aid of China had been agreed to fill in the time before 'Anakim', since marking time in Burma for nearly a year, if acceptable to British planners, was anathema to Roosevelt. Churchill could leave Casablanca feeling that he had reestablished British standing in the war against Japan in American eyes. On the 25th, after the conclusion of the conference, remembering that some American hearts were best reached via Chungking, he sent Chiang a telegram pledging continued British assistance against Japan once Germany was beaten.[46]

Whatever minimal clarity had been attained at Casablanca quickly dissolved in its aftermath, however. The President moved closer to giving Chennault priority over Stilwell, without altering his desire for land operations in Burma, while the doubts expressed tentatively at Casablanca by the Joint Planning Staff about the value of reopening the Burma Road hardened into certainty in London, and events elsewhere made 'Anakim' as improbable in November 1943 as its predecessor a year before. On 14 February Chennault became a major general and the China Air Task Force became the Fourteenth United States Air Force, which not only enhanced its commander's standing but freed him from Stilwell's control and placed him directly under Washington. Slowly but surely Roosevelt was veering away from the War Department-Stilwell plan for a great Americanized Chinese army.[47] When Anthony Eden visited Washington a month later, the President scribbled a note during an evening of discussion at the White House: ' "Anakim" out. Keep China going by air.'[48] Perhaps Roosevelt's political instincts had begun to warn him that his original China strategy was built upon sand. So loosely organized was wartime Washington, however, that as late as April the War Shipping Administration was offering the British twenty ships for 'Anakim' and the Joint Chiefs of Staff were pressing their British opposite numbers for more vigour in preparing it.[49]

Meanwhile, General H. H. Arnold, the commanding general of the USAAF, and Field-Marshal Sir John Dill had been in Delhi and Chungking to explain the Casablanca decisions and investigate ways of increasing the Hump airlift to support Chennault, a mission that reflected the ambiguity Roosevelt had introduced into allied strategy in the area. Stilwell believed the British were simply bluffing about 'Anakim'. When Dill described the plan in general terms to Chiang, the Generalissimo, who had hitherto been one of 'Anakim's' principal supporters, cabled Churchill that the great need was to improve the capacity of the Hump airlift before Chinese armies could play their part in 'Anakim', which the Prime Minister assured him would be done.[50] By this time, however, 'Anakim's' prospects looked very bleak.

The basic premise on which the 'Anakim' plan was built was the availability of enough shipping to build up the forces in India, as well as to maintain the import programme vital to the functioning of the Indian economy. On 18 January 1943 the Quartermaster-General of the British Army estimated the needs of 'Anakim' at forty ships a month, and the following month in Delhi Wavell's discussions with Arnold and Dill assumed that 183,000 tons of shipping a month would be allotted to the build-up for 'Anakim'. But the massive shipping losses sustained by the alliance since American entry into the war led to a serious crisis, threatening not only to disrupt allied strategy but also the import programme on which the economy and war production of the United Kingdom itself depended. In November 1942, Roosevelt had promised that the provision of enough American shipping to maintain a 27 million-ton import programme – the lowest of the war – would enjoy 'absolute' priority. But such was the decentralization prevailing in Washington that it was not until Eden's visit in March that the President finally imposed that priority on the American military. In February, despite a warning a month earlier from the Viceroy that the food situation in India was ominous, Churchill had minuted to Lord Leathers, the Minister of War Transport, 'there is no reason why all parts of the British Empire should not feel the pinch in the same way as the Mother Country has done', and sailings to the Indian Ocean were steadily cut – from an average of one hundred a month in the first half of 1942, to eighty by the end of the year, then a sharp cut of 50 percent, to forty a month early in 1943.[51] These cuts alone would have been enough to finish 'Anakim', but the longer the planners in Delhi and London looked at it, the less they liked it.

Churchill had returned to London after his post-Casablanca mission to Turkey, keen to pursue 'Anakim'. He ordered the creation of a special planning group to 'keep the heat steadily turned on this great operation, and to inform COS Committee and me from week to week how everything is going, what can be done to make it work, and of any hitches.'[52] The previous day, however, Wavell had cabled home a report of the conferences held in Delhi and Calcutta with Dill, Arnold, Stilwell and Chinese representatives. Three points in this cable were crucial: the figure of 183,000 tons of shipping per month for 'Anakim' was essential, the bulk of the supplies and equipment would have to be shipped from the US or Britain by June in order to allow time for training before the new 'Anakim' target date of 15 November, and, even if all this was provided the RAF commander in India, Air Chief Marshal Sir Richard Pierse, still did not believe he would have the resources to allow an operational tempo that would clear Burma in one campaigning season.[53] That, in turn, put the reconquest of Burma and the opening of the Burma Road off until 1944-45. At this point Wavell clearly lost his taste for 'Anakim'. On the 16th he sent a note to his planning staff which again reveals him at his most imaginative. He suggested that there could be no element of surprise in any attack on Burma, and that the natural obstacles were so formidable that 'we may have to look elsewhere for a speedy and effective blow against the Japanese line . . . The objective I have in mind for such a blow is the control of the Sunda Straits between Sumatra and Java. This would threaten Singapore and the whole Japanese position in the Netherlands East Indies. If we could at the same time seize a base in northern Sumatra from which to control the Malacca Straits, we should have gone far towards the defeat of Japan.'[54] In his note to his chief of staff the previous April, Wavell had suggested that an amphibious operation against northern Sumatra was worth examining. Now, convinced that 'Anakim' was a non-starter, he swung back to a wide-ranging amphibious strategy, not unlike the 'island-hopping' procedure subsequently used by the Americans in the Pacific.

The problem with Wavell's ideas was that the resources needed for them would exceed even those for 'Anakim', which the British had been unable to find by themselves. There were also political complications. An adept at strategic deception, Wavell felt that Chinese interest in Burma, and poor Chinese security, could be used, in conjunction with minor operations, to keep Japanese attention riveted on Burma.[55] He ignored, as he had been wont to do, the much greater political problem posed by American interest in Burma.

By this time, the Prime Minister was becoming impatient with the vista of problems and delays that cables from Delhi were revealing, complaining to Ismay that 'all our operations are being spoiled by overloading and playing for safety as a certainty . . . The "Anakim" demands are altogether excessive.'[56] But now the Joint Planning Staff, which Churchill once described as 'the machinery of negation', came down decisively against 'Anakim'. In January they had indicated some doubts about the feasibility of mounting it before the end of the war in Europe, then projected for December, 1944. After studying the cables from the commanders in Delhi, they came to the conclusion that the importance of the Burma Road had been much overrated. It had, after all, only been capable of carrying, at most, 400 tons a day in peacetime, and, if it was not reopened until 1945, it would make little appreciable contribution to the war against Japan, whose end was projected for 1946. 600 aircraft on the Hump route could lift as much as the Road, allow the Fourteenth Air Force to attempt Chennault's plan, and bolster Chinese morale. Operations in Burma could then be scaled down to the capture of Akyab and a limited offensive in the north. British efforts could be more profitably employed in an operation against northern Sumatra.[57] Like Wavell, the Joint Planning Staff were ignoring the question of resources. They were also, like him, missing the point, because the governing factor in Burma, although the British clearly did not yet fully grasp it, was not their military logic but American concern about China.

The Chiefs of Staff and the Prime Minister accepted the logic of the Joint Planning Staff argument against 'Anakim' by mid-April, and began contemplating a more far-flung amphibious strategy. But at that moment, the only British offensive operation

of the 1942-43 dry season, an attempt to take Akyab by an overland advance along the Arakan coast, was collapsing ignominiously.
Churchill had followed its progress closely, and, as it first stalled
and then collapsed, the tone of his minutes became steadily more
waspish.[58] He realized that the psychological and political effect
of what he described at a Chiefs of Staff meeting as 'this
lamentable scene' were far more important than the failure to
reach a military objective of diminishing importance. April, 1943
marked the nadir of British fortunes in the war against Japan.
On the 9th, the commanders in India, Wavell and Pierse, as well
as Admiral Sir James Somerville, Commander-in-Chief, Eastern
Fleet, were summoned home for 'consultations'.

(iii)

The first Arakan campaign, perhaps the worst managed British
military effort of the war, was the deformed offspring of the
1942 'Anakim' plan. An amphibious assault on Akyab ('Cannibal')
was originally scheduled for the autumn of 1942, to seize an airfield from which the RAF could cover the subsequent assault on
Rangoon. As 'Anakim' was slowly eroded, 'Cannibal' changed
from a subsidiary operation to India Command's principal offensive activity for the 1942-43 dry season. On 17 November 1942
Wavell cancelled the amphibious assault on Akyab and two days
later ordered an overland advance down the Arakan coast to seize
a jumping off place at the tip of the Mayu peninsula for a subsequent assault on Akyab by a locally improvised fleet of small
craft. With 'Anakim' cancelled and the limited offensive in north
Burma ('Ravenous') that was to complement it literally washed
out by the monsoon, the alternative to a truncated 'Cannibal'
was to do nothing until 1943-44. Wavell felt that both the morale
of the Indian Army and the prestige of the Raj required some demonstration of offensive capacity before then. Furthermore,
there were good tactical reasons for an advance on Akyab. Success would sharply reduce the Japanese air threat to the industrial region around Calcutta, provide a forward air base to cover
a post-monsoon 'Anakim', and erode Japanese air strength in
Burma. Major-General W. T. Lloyd's 14th Division, which had
been inching down the coast since September, was therefore committed to a frontal assault against the Japanese and some of the
worst terrain in Burma.[59]

However logical the reasons for the first Arakan campaign may have seemed in Delhi, it was in fact one of Wavell's worst mistakes. The RAF in India, although growing in strength, still had no fighter that was a match for the Japanese Zero. Any air battles were, therefore, more likely to erode British than Japanese strength.[60] Moreover, politically desirable as success was, the Indian Army was not yet capable of providing it. When Japan entered the war, India had more troops serving overseas than any other country of the British Empire, many rushed out of India incompletely trained and equipped to meet imperial needs in the east or west. In January 1942, Leopold Amery, the Secretary of State for India and Burma, placed before his cabinet colleagues a paper in which he made plain the dimensions of the Indian war effort. 264,000 men were serving overseas. An armoured division, a motor brigade and five infantry divisions were in the Middle East, three divisions were in Malaya and likely to be lost there, and another division was in Burma. Amery also underlined the cost of this effort.

> India has invariably been better than her promises in meeting demands for the despatch of troops overseas well before the dates by which it had been undertaken that they would be ready . . . by the use of every expedient and improvisation during training . . . units have only received sufficient weapons, by no means the full scale, after orders to proceed overseas have been issued.

At the time, Amery wrote, India was organizing the remaining four divisions of the 1941 programme plus one left over from 1940, while trying to remain on schedule with the 1942 programme, which called for another five. Simultaneously, newly raised administrative units were being steadily pulled out of India, which made the task of turning collections of raw infantry battalions into divisions even harder.[61]

The 14th Indian Division was part of the 1941 expansion programme. It lost its 63rd Brigade to Burma early in 1942. By March 1942 it was brought up to strength again with units taken from the North-West Frontier and scraped up from internal security duties. At the same time two new divisions of the 1942 programme were formed. When the first Burma campaign ended in May, the 14th, in common with most Indian Army divisions, still had only half its authorized scale of equipment. During the summer of 1942, one of the 1942 programme divisions was broken up to rebuild the 17th Division and to transform the 1st Burma Division into the 39th Indian Division, but the raising of a third armoured division was begun and a new divisional headquarters was formed to handle the amphibious training that the burgeoning offensive projects demanded. Thus, throughout the summer of 1942 the Indian Army, still desperately short of equipment, continued to grow, with the inevitable dilution, cross-postings and shuffling of units between formations that was entailed. The supply of 'martial class' recruits for further expansion was at an end; many new units came from outside the Indian Army family circle and the experiment of welding the newcomers into the Army by cross-posting VCOs from older northern units to new Madrassi battalions was not a success. Technical specialists of all kinds were in short supply, while for an army that would campaign in a country where malaria was endemic, the shortage of doctors was particularly alarming. There were only 14,000 medical practitioners in all of India, and more of them had already been called up by early 1942 than during the entire First World War. It was a very shaky force with which Wavell set out to capture Akyab.[62]

He made the task more difficult by allowing it to be managed by a very clumsy command structure, something that was becoming almost a hallmark of British operations in the east. Wavell retained overall control but operational control was vested in Eastern Army, commanded by Lieutenant-General N. M. S. Irwin, whose headquarters were at Ranchi in Bihar. Irwin in turn controlled Lieutenant-General Geoffrey Scoones's IV Corps in Assam and Lloyd's 14th Division in the Arakan. Irwin (like Wavell) was not an Indian Army officer, and his considerable abilities were flawed by an overbearing and insensitive temperament. He had greeted Burcorps on its arrival in Assam with an Order of the Day that implied the loss of Burma was due to a lack of fighting spirit, and when Slim had protested at his manner, Irwin had replied, 'I can't be rude, I'm senior.'[63] Lloyd's division had originally been part of Slim's XV Corps, whose headquarters were alongside those of Eastern Army at Ranchi. The 14th Division's original role, when it started on its way down the Arakan coast in September, was simply to divert Japanese attention and to draw formations out of Akyab before the amphibious assault, and Irwin's decision to keep Lloyd directly under his headquarters is understandable. When the amphibious attack was cancelled, however, and 14th Division's advance became Eastern Army's only operation, Irwin's failure to insert a corps headquarters between himself and Lloyd became a serious problem.

Despite all handicaps, Lloyd had almost reached the tip of the Mayu peninsula by the end of 1942, but the Japanese, who understood the value of Akyab and who were not pressed on any other front in Burma, were now reinforcing as rapidly as they could. The two battalions that had initially faced Lloyd were awaiting the arrival of a fresh division, while Lloyd's troops, at the end of a four-month advance and a long precarious supply line, were stalled just short of their objective by a cleverly sited and stubbornly held Japanese bunker complex. Under pressure from Wavell, Irwin now began to feed reinforcements to Lloyd, who had started with four brigades, instead of the normal three. Eventually Lloyd's single divisional headquarters was trying to control nine brigades, with disastrous results. Although drawing forces from XV Corps, Irwin ignored Slim's headquarters, asking no advice from the one general in India experienced in fighting the Japanese, and ignoring sound advice that was volunteered. Irwin, of course, was under great pressure from Wavell, whose deficiencies became progressively sharper as he descended from theatre command to actual conduct of operations. Wavell, by this time a very tired man, had never fought the Japanese himself and continued to regard them as badly overrated.[64] In his 'Operation Fantastical' paper of September 1942, he had written of his 'hunch' that, if pushed, the Japanese would retreat; he said much the same thing to Irwin in January 1943.[65] As late as 26 February, despite mounting indications that the Japanese were preparing a counter-attack, Wavell was pressing Irwin to order Lloyd to smash the Japanese in front of the 14th Division by sheer weight of numbers. Shortly after Lloyd's final effort on 18 March, the Japanese struck back.

The British collapse in the Arakan over the next month was as bad as anything that had happened in Malaya or Burma. The only compensation, as Churchill noted sarcastically the day before he ordered Wavell home, was that the relatively small scale of the operations kept them from attracting much public notice.

Irwin, having put Lloyd in an impossible position, sacked him on 29 March when, in the face of orders to the contrary from the Army commander, Lloyd began a withdrawal from his forward positions on the Mayu peninsula. Irwin briefly controlled operations himself then, on 14 April – much too late – he did what ought to have been done months before and brought in Slim's corps headquarters. All Slim could do was manage the retirement of the battered Indian units to their original start line, where they settled down in monsoon positions at the end of May.

Ample evidence of the low state of morale among both British and Indian troops in the final stages of the campaign shook everyone from Wavell down. 'Has there been any surrender without fighting or desertion to the enemy by Indian troops?' Wavell wrote to Irwin on 9 April. 'I am more worried about the morale aspect both of the troops and to India [sic] than anything else.'[66] In fact British and Indian morale was equally bad. Some British units (like the battalions of the 6th brigade of the 2nd British division, committed in March) were new to India, others had perhaps been in the east far too long. On at least two occasions British battalions fell apart in something like panic. Many of the Indian troops were in an equally bad state. Poorly trained and terrified of the jungle, patrols, unless accompanied by a British officer, would simply lie up and return after a suitable interval to report that they had seen nothing. On one occasion a critical position was lost because its jittery defenders had fired off all their ammunition at night noises in the jungle. One unit refused an order to advance, another threw away its rifles during a retirement, and, perhaps not surprisingly, 'defeatist and disloyal' talk was reported rife among the wounded. One of Slim's liaison officers summed it up well: 'the seasoned and highly trained Jap troops are confronted by a force which, although impressive on paper, is little better, in a large number of cases, than a rather unwilling band of raw levies.'[67] Irwin himself after the campaign estimated that British and Indian troops were worth only half their number of Japanese in the jungle – and they were in fact beaten by about half their number of Japanese.[68] Slim himself, four days after taking over, wrote that his British troops were 'browned off', while many of his Indian troops, especially recent drafts, were inferior in physique, training and morale. The force as a whole had one battle left in it. 'We are fighting an army in which the best men go into the Infantry, and we shan't make much progress until we follow suit,' he concluded.[69] As the dismal tale of disaster in the Arakan came to an end, it was counterpointed by a brief welcome flash of offensive brilliance – the first Chindit operation.

Lieutenant-Colonel Orde Charles Wingate, who, in little more than a year from the beginning of the first Chindit expedition, won great fame, created a legend, and sparked controversies that endure to this day, arrived in India in early March 1942 at Wavell's request. Wingate, a gunner and distant relative of T. E. Lawrence, had discovered his vocation for irregular warfare in Palestine during the 1936-38 Arab Revolt, when he had organized the 'Special Night Squads' from among Jewish settlers to combat Arab raiders (Moshe Dayan was one of his recruits). Although his fanatical attachment to Zionism, his odd personality, and his unorthodox military ideas did not endear him to many colleagues and most superiors, he impressed Wavell, who was GOC in Palestine in 1936-37. Under Wavell's reserved exterior lurked an affinity with the odd and unorthodox which surfaced time and again – most importantly in connection with Wingate. The beginning of the war found Wingate rusticated as brigade major of an anti-aircraft unit in Kent. After Italy entered the war, Leopold Amery, whose strategic imagination was almost as sweeping as Wavell's, suggested that Wingate had the ideal combination of talent and personality to direct irregular operations inside Italian-occupied Ethiopia. Wavell welcomed the suggestion, and in October 1940 Wingate left for Cairo. There followed a hectic eight months organizing and leading Ethiopian irregulars against the demoralized and disintegrating Italian forces and their local levies – and, characteristically, engaging in furious arguments with a variety of British officers. At the end Wingate suffered a nervous collapse in Cairo, during which he attempted suicide. Shipped home to England, by any normal standards his career was over. Then, for the third time, fate, in the form of Wavell, intervened. Wingate did a hurried reconnaissance of upper Burma in the company of the commandant of the School of Bush Warfare, Major Michael Calvert, in March 1942, but the collapse in Burma was too rapid for him to organize any operations there. His previous experience and what he had seen in Burma went into a series of memoranda he wrote in Delhi in April and May, which, with Wavell's support, became the starting point of the Long Range Penetration Groups – the Chindits. Wingate believed that wireless communications and air power together presented revolutionary possibilities. He proposed to operate a force of specially trained and organized regular troops behind enemy lines in Burma, depending on radio to coordinate their movements and arrange resupply by air. Such a force could disrupt Japanese communications and supply intelligence. At this point Wingate made no claim that LRP groups could become the means of reconquering Burma – that came later. Originally they were to operate in advance of a IV Corps offensive from Assam. In July 1942, the new force, known as the 77th Indian Infantry Brigade, began training in central India.[70]

Wingate's force was composed of three battalions: the 13th King's Liverpool Regiment, a wartime unit that had reached India in 1941 and been on garrison and internal security duties since, the 3/2nd Gurkha Rifles, a wartime expansion unit with few regular officers, and a Burma Rifles battalion, composed largely of hillmen, one of the few Burma Rifle units that had lasted out the whole retreat. To these were added a commando unit and RAF signallers. Wingate's champions, who seem to share their hero's single-mindedness, have made much of the quality of the troops provided, alleging deliberate efforts at sabotage by hostile orthodox soldiers in Delhi. But in May and June 1942 there was only one complete British division available in India, and the shaky military situation on the eastern frontier, allied to the looming political crisis in India itself, made its disruption unwise. The six British battalions that came out with Burcorps, while experienced, were the merest skeletons, needing prolonged convalescence. Enough has already been said to make it clear that good Indian battalions were equally scarce, and even a new Gurkha unit had considerable value to the Indian Army. Wingate had a tendency, common among pioneers of new methods in military institutions, to see anything less than wholehearted support as rampant hostility. While he did not get crack battalions, neither did any other newly raised formation in India. The basic unit in Wingate's brigade was the column, based on a British or Gurkha company, with the RAF signallers, commando personnel, and members of the Burma Rifles who would provide guides and interpreters, added. There were seven columns, organized in two groups, and by early 1943 they were poised in Assam, ready to strike. By then, however, the whole framework within which they were to be employed had collapsed.

When Wavell approved the formation of the 77th Brigade, he cherished hopes of an autumn offensive that would combine limited operations in north Burma ('Ravenous') with amphibious assaults on Akyab and Rangoon. By the time the LRP formation was ready, all this had dwindled into 14th Division's ill-fated advance on Akyab. To launch Wingate's formation into Burma on its own seemed so hazardous that Wavell flew up from Delhi to Imphal in Assam in early February prepared to cancel the operation. Wingate, who did not lack eloquence, pleaded for the chance to try his theories, correctly sensing that it was then or never for him. Wavell, whose optimism about forcing a Japanese withdrawal has already been noted, and who believed, as he had written the previous September, in unorthodox approaches to the problem of Burma, decided that the experience to be gained made the gamble worthwhile. On 8 February 1943, the Chindits left Imphal.

Crossing the Chindwin River into Burma, Wingate's columns struck east and, early in March, succeeded in demolishing the Mandalay-Myitkyina railway at several points. Up to this point the Chindits had been largely successful in evading the Japanese, and casualties had been light. Now, in a departure from his original plan, Wingate carried his force across the Irrawaddy, into largely waterless terrain easily sealed off by the now aroused Japanese. Forced to break up into small 'dispersal groups', the Chindits made their way back to India over the next few months. Of the 3,000 men who left Imphal about 2,200 returned, most of them unfit for further LRP operations. Chindit I, small and costly as it was, nevertheless made three important contributions to the future of the war in Burma. The first was the practical demonstration it gave of the possibilities of air supply and the techniques necessary to operate it. The Japanese suffered little but transient damage, but they began to examine again the security of their western flank, and this review was one of the factors that led to their disastrous 1943-44 offensives. Perhaps the most important result of Chindit I, however, was its psychological impact and the consequent reverberations at the highest levels of alliance politics. The Chindits had gone into Burma, operated successfully, if at a high cost, and come out again. This, coming at precisely the moment of the Arakan debacle, proved to be the decisive factor for the future of British strategy in the war against Japan.[71]

Failure in the Arakan had discredited Wavell and the Indian Army with Churchill, who had never had very great confidence in either. Wingate had provided a flash of what could be described as success, and he and his romantic, bearded Chindits provided the first authentic touch of glamour in a war that had so far lacked both. However disliked Wingate may have been in Delhi, correspondents and public relations officers were desperate for good news from Burma in May 1943, and Wingate quickly became the best known soldier in India, and an instant celebrity in Britain. Churchill, although he had many differences with Wavell, shared his enthusiasm for unusual approaches to military problems, as well as his affinity for romantic figures. He also needed success in the Far East. Wingate was a godsend. A copy of Wingate's report on Chindit I reached Amery early in July and was passed on to Churchill. The Prime Minister had already resolved to replace Wavell, and now his mind turned to sending out Lieutenant-General Sir Oliver Leese, with Wingate under him as operational commander in Burma. On 24 July he sent an acid minute to Ismay. 'There is no doubt that in the welter of lassitude and inefficiency that has characterized our operations on the Indian front, this man, his force and achievements, stand out . . .'[72] The following day Wingate was summoned home.

III

Trident and Quadrant: the Final Decisions on Burma May–September 1943

(i)

The failure of the Arakan offensive reinforced doubts that had been developing in Delhi and London about the wisdom of re-taking Burma by a direct assault, and a strong move arose to bypass Burma by striking east and south across the Bay of Bengal. Because this promised no direct help to China, it ran directly counter to American interests, thus posing the possibility of a breach in the unity of the alliance. When this Anglo-American impasse was resolved in the late summer of 1943, the solution was a characteristically ambiguous one. American interest in clearing Burma was written into alliance strategy, while the British – especially the Prime Minister – continued to hope and plan for a very different strategy against Japan, one that would avoid all but minor operations in Burma.

Wavell, as we have seen, had been growing dubious about the reconquest of Burma since at least February. In mid-April Irwin sent a 'Note On Our Capacity To Operate Offensively Against Burma' to Wavell, Morris, and Pierse that reinforced the com-mander-in-chief's doubts on the eve of his departure for London. 'The very limited operations carried out this year have disclosed the lamentable fact that the Army is not yet sufficiently trained or efficiently led [sic] to take on the Japanese on even superior terms in numbers or material,' Irwin wrote, with unselfconscious irony. The conclusion he drew was that, since resources were adequate only for building up either the army or the air force, the latter should receive priority in 1943-44, while the former confined itself to 'aggressive defence'. Only in 1944-45 would the army be ready to go over to the offensive.[1] In London the Joint Planning Staff had been thinking along similar lines and on the 15th the War Cabinet, on their advice, cancelled 'Anakim'. A week later Churchill presided over a Chiefs' of Staff committee meeting at which the newly arrived commanders-in-chief from

India were present for the first time, and he set the tone for a new direction in British strategy against Japan.

> The Prime Minister said that undoubtedly the best way to defeat the Japanese was by bombing Japan from bases in Russia and China. This could not, however, be undertaken until after the defeat of Germany. Meanwhile, he was inclined to think that we should concentrate on the support of China by the largest possible air transport service and find the most favourable locality for attacking the Japanese, 'bypassing' Burma, and making full use of our seapower.[2]

With that Churchill took his departure, suggesting that the Chiefs of Staff discuss the matter with Wavell, Pierse, and Somerville. The following day the Chiefs of Staff asked the Joint Planning Staff for studies on the British contribution to the defeat of Japan and the desirability of further operations in Burma as a means to that end. It is an indication of the degree to which opinion had hardened among the planners that the papers were ready four days later. The Joint Planning Staff agreed that Russian entry would be decisive but in the meantime the first step was for Britain and the United States to agree on their policy for the war in the east. They suggested that the severance of Japanese sea communications was the quickest way to victory, and to that end the British should 'plan for operations to re-capture the Japanese sources of oil from the west when Germany has been defeated'. Further operations in Burma they dismissed as 'unlikely to further our ultimate object – the defeat of Japan – to an extent commensurate with the cost.' In their second paper they amplified their reasons for rejecting a major effort to clear Burma. They did not believe that the Burma Road could ever be a major factor in Chinese resistance, and felt a reinforced airlift would do all that was either necessary or possible to sustain China. The only military activity they could recommend in Burma was minor operations in the north to protect the air route, improve the training of the Indian Army, and keep some pressure on the Japanese. With 'Anakim' cancelled they did not foresee any major operations based on India during the 1943-44 dry season. They had come, by a somewhat different path, to the same conclusion as Irwin: no major British contribution to the war against Japan was possible before 1944-45. Within forty-eight hours of the completion of these papers they had been approved by the Chiefs of Staff and the War Cabinet.[3]

The day after the War Cabinet agreed that nothing significant could be done against Japan for at least fifteen months, Amery, who was not a member of that body, wrote a minute for Churchill, sparked, in part at least, by exchanges with Field-Marshal J. C. Smuts, the South African Prime Minister. Amery of course was fully aware of the disillusionment in India and Whitehall with operations in Burma and repeated the now standard argument against any further effort there. Unlike Irwin and the Joint Planners, he did not, however, recommend marking time for a year. For 1943-44 he advocated a much expanded use of Long Range Penetration Groups in Burma, coupled with an amphibious operation against northern Sumatra, which he rather curiously described as a feint. Amery (and Smuts) believed that the most deadly thrust at Japan would be a blow at Thailand or Indochina to seize bases from which Japan's maritime lifelines could be assailed, and for 1944-45 he proposed a landing on the Kra Isthmus, followed by either a converging attack on Singapore in conjunction with the force from Sumatra, or a drive north on Bangkok.[4] This blended reasonably well with Churchill's own views, for, although he agreed with the general trend of staff thinking on Burma, he had not yet accepted that nothing ambitious could be mounted from the Indian base until 1944-45. Amery's paper also reached the Prime Minister at a moment when he had both the inclination and the enforced leisure in which to concentrate on the war against Japan.

The American Chiefs of Staff were unhappy with both current and future prospects in Burma. So were Chiang and Stilwell, while the priority to be accorded to the latter's operations, as opposed to Chennault's, was still unclear. Stilwell and Chennault were both in Washington to argue their respective cases, and the commanders-in-chief from India were invited to return from London by way of the United States for a discussion of future prospects. Churchill was not keen on this, but realized that politically he could not refuse. He had no intention, however, of letting Britain be represented by Wavell, inarticulate, and not overly pro-American, in whom the Prime Minister's confidence had ebbed away and whom he had made up his mind to replace. Churchill, therefore, told the War Cabinet that he and the Chiefs of Staff would also go to Washington.[5] In any case, the future of operations in the Mediterranean had not yet been decided, nor had the relationship between them and the cross-channel attack, and neither Churchill nor Brooke intended to allow their European priorities to be affected by the American obsession with China. The Prime Minister, who had had pneumonia in February, was forbidden to fly by his doctors, so on 4 May he left London for the Clyde and sailed the next day on the *Queen Mary*.

Two concerns dominated Churchill's thinking about the Japanese war. One was future command arrangements in India; the second was a strategic formulation that would both satisfy the Americans and avoid an overland reconquest of Burma. The former proved easier by far to settle. Wavell clearly was out. He had borne tremendous responsibilities since he took over as commander-in-chief in the Middle East on the eve of the war. By the spring of 1943 he was very tired, his touch unsure, and his ability to work easily in harness with the Americans suspect. On the other hand, he could not simply be sacked. Fortunately for the Prime Minister, a convenient solution to the dilemma of pushing Wavell quietly aside came to hand almost immediately. The Marquess of Linlithgow had been Viceroy since 1936. His term had been extended once, in 1940, but he was as tired as Wavell and a replacement had to be found. The problem was finding a suitable man. Everyone, except possibly Churchill, realized that the Raj would come to an end in the aftermath of victory; in any case, the Viceroyalty had rarely assisted any ambitious politician's career, and there was no queue of candidates. Amery suggested Eden, who demurred, as did Oliver Lyttleton, the Minister of Production. The names of Sir John Anderson, Lord President of the Council and a former Governor of Bengal, as well as that of Gwilym Lloyd George, the Minister of Fuel and Power, appeared briefly. In the end, after reaching Washington, Wavell's name was suggested and, although the Prime Minister was not immediately receptive, the way to disembarrass himself of Wavell was now available.[6] Command arrangements were secondary, however, to the fundamental problem of what the commander was to do. On the voyage to America, Churchill asked the Chiefs of Staff to examine Amery's proposals. Their sweep obviously appealed to him because he

believed that if the Americans were faced with a British decision
to drop Burma, it would be more palatable to them if the British at
the same time presented a grand design for the war in South-East
Asia: 'It is not really much use feeding them with morsels like
Akyab and Ramree Island, palatable though they may be.'[7] 'My
own impression,' he wrote in another paper, 'is that the Americans will require to be satisfied that the maximum action is taken
in this theatre, and that it is not being displaced in importance in
our minds . . .' He then went on to develop some ideas of his
own for a British grand design in the east. He began by admitting
'I cannot pretend to have given any thought to the problem up
to the present or to be properly acquainted with its salient
features,' but he went on to tackle the question of 'how . . . are
we to come to grips with Japan in 1945 and 1946.' Clearly he
was working on the premise that the German war would be over
by the end of 1944, and the rest of his paper was an imaginative
fusion of many of the ideas developed in previous discussions in
London, with a few touches of his own. The crucial blow at
Japan would be delivered from the Pacific, Churchill wrote, reflecting the consensus reached by Wavell and his planners, the
Joint Planning Staff, and the Chiefs of Staff, that nothing decisive could be accomplished in Burma. He then picked up the
idea about Russian participation mentioned in the Joint Planners'
paper and developed the ingenious argument that a Russian
entry into the war, complementing Pacific operations, would seal
Japan's doom, and that this desirable goal could best be promoted
by a concentration of effort on defeating Germany. This may
have been aimed at encouraging Brooke, who resolutely opposed
any Asian commitment that would eat into the resources available
for the European war, to view the paper favourably. Churchill
admitted, however, that this line of argument would have to be
deployed carefully, lest Marshall use it to reinforce his own
predilection for closing down Mediterranean operations entirely
in favour of the cross-channel attack. Coming to specific British
operations in lieu of Burma, he made the ideas expressed at
various times by Wavell, Amery and the Joint Planners his own,
calling for amphibious operations across the Bay of Bengal and
suggesting possible targets along a great arc from Moulmein to
Timor. The Prime Minister felt that such an operation could be
launched early in 1944, without waiting for the end of the

European war.[8] He thus embraced Amery's timetable and the Joint Planners' conclusions. Brooke strongly disagreed and in the end a compromise was reached, by which the operations Churchill wanted would be taken under study by the planners.[9] The British arrived in Washington therefore imperfectly united. Everyone agreed that the reconquest of Burma was unnecessary to victory over Japan, and that an increased airlift, assisted by minor operations in north Burma to secure for it a safer, more convenient route, would answer the purposes of sustaining China. They were also agreed that the most rewarding use of British power was in a maritime and amphibious offensive south-east across the Bay of Bengal with the aim of severing Japan from the resources of the southern region of its empire. However, the Chiefs of Staff, led by Brooke, could see no hope of doing this before 1944-45, whereas Churchill wanted something on the agenda for 1943-44. The Prime Minister's instinct proved sounder, politically if not militarily, for the weakness of Brooke's position was that it left the 1943-44 campaigning season empty, a gap into which Burma could be pushed by the Americans.

The Trident Conference centred on two Anglo-American clashes. The most important, over the relationship between further Mediterranean operations after 'Husky', the invasion of Sicily scheduled for July, and the invasion of north-west Europe, produced separate British and American position papers on 17 and 18 May and was finally resolved by a compromise that reflected the changing balance of power in the alliance. The cross-channel attack, the operation closest to Marshall's heart, was finally given a specific target date (1 May 1944). In return the Americans agreed to the planning of 'such operations in exploitation of "Husky" as are best calculated to eliminate Italy from the War and to contain the maximum number of German forces.' However, final approval of any Mediterranean operation was reserved to the Combined Chiefs of Staff, which preserved American veto power and gave them considerable leverage against the British. It was also agreed that after 1 November 1943 four American and three British divisions (20 percent of the total force in the theatre) would be withdrawn from the Mediterranean to the United Kingdom to prepare for the invasion of France. The firm British determination to preserve their Mediterranean options was the background against which the second argument over future strategy in the Far East took place.

14 May, with the battle over the Mediterranean versus north-west Europe looming, was the decisive day for Far Eastern matters at 'Trident'. In the morning there was a mammoth session of the Combined Chiefs of Staff, with Chennault, Stilwell, Wavell, Pierse, and Somerville in attendance. Wavell, supported by Brooke, argued the British case against further operations in Burma, which amounted to a British endorsement of Chennault's strategy. Stilwell evaded British arguments about the time required to develop the Burma Road, and its low carrying capacity, by claiming that its psychological effect on the Chinese was so important that it had to be reopened for that reason alone. Admiral William Leahy, Roosevelt's personal Chief of Staff, supported Stilwell. The Joint Chiefs of Staff still considered China of paramount importance. Faith in the offensive capacity of rejuvenated Chinese armies was beginning to wane in Washington, but in its place was the vision of China as the platform for an air offensive that would batter Japan prior to the final invasion – and would incidentally give the United States Army Air Force a role in the defeat of Japan independent of the Navy-dominated Central Pacific and Army-controlled South-West Pacific theatres. For this to happen, however, China had to remain in the war, and it had now become dogma in the United States that reopening the Burma Road was essential to continued Chinese belligerency. Even Chiang's declining credit would not free the British from the incubus of the Road. The Anglo-American dialogue continued after an adjournment for lunch. Stillwell had already suggested a limited offensive to clear north Burma and open the way for the Ledo Road to be driven through to Yunnan. Wavell had argued against such an operation on the triple grounds that Assam was a nearly impossible administrative base for an offensive; that, if an offensive was nevertheless launched, its demands would sharply reduce the amount that could be carried forward to the Assam bases of the China airlift; and that, even if launched and successful, building 250 miles of all-weather road into Yunnan before the 1944 monsoon was impossible, since the roadbuilders' material would have to come over the Assam line of communications which would already be clogged with supplies for both the offensive and the airlift.

For good measure Wavell added that a quarter of the force involved would fall victim to malaria. Nothing daunted, Roosevelt summed up the day's discussions by announcing that the allied objective in South-East Asia was an airlift of 7,000 tons a month by July and the reopening of the Burma Road. Churchill, although he had growled at Stilwell that he had no intention of doing something absurd simply to placate Chiang, entered no objection. Despite their resolution to avoid further operations in Burma, the British were again committed to going into the water to fight the shark, in the Prime Minister's picturesque phrase.[10]

Churchill and Brooke acquiesced for several reasons. In the first place they had a much more important battle pending over the Mediterranean which they meant to win. The Prime Minister had recognized, even before Pearl Harbour, that Japan was primarily an American responsibility, and he knew all too well that China was not an arguable subject with the Americans (any more than India was with him). Furthermore, British strength at previous conferences with the Americans came not only from their preponderant contribution to the war but also from their unity behind carefully prepared positions. At 'Trident' British preponderance was on the wane and, as far as the war with Japan was concerned, the Prime Minister and his advisers were not unified except in their dislike of operations in Burma. Churchill wanted an Asian 'Torch' mounted against northern Sumatra in 1944, while Brooke and the other Chiefs did not think it was practical. Having nothing of their own to propose, the British were ill-positioned to resist the Americans who were both clear about what they wanted and determined to get it.

In the final report by the Combined Chiefs to the President and the Prime Minister, the British committed themselves to raising the airlift to 10,000 tons a month by the autumn, 'vigorous and aggressive' operations in north Burma during the 1943-44 dry season 'as an essential step toward the opening of the Burma Road', and amphibious operations to capture Akyab and Ramree. Despite Stilwell's demand, on behalf of the Chinese, that the British resuscitate 'Anakim' and reconquer all of Burma as an act of good faith, the final formulation left an opening for Churchill's preferred strategy, for India Command was directed to continue preparations 'for the eventual launching of an overseas operation of about the size of "Anakim",' but the object of the expedition was not specified.[11] Another gleam of hope for British proponents of an amphibious strategy came in the paper the Joint Chiefs of Staff gave their British opposite numbers, setting out their strategy for the final defeat of Japan. To supplement the Burma Road, they proposed to seize Hong Kong, approaching it via the Philippines. A British advance through the Straits of Malacca would be complementary to this, forcing a wide dispersal of Japanese strength.[12] Taken as a whole, however, the final act of the 'Trident' conference bore out Churchill's prediction: 'I was sure that our American friends would be very anxious that we should do everything possible – and even impossible – in the way of immediate operations from India.'[13]

From Washington, the Prime Minister flew to North Africa, accompanied by Marshall, to try to get agreement on the post 'Husky' operations he had fought so hard to make possible. But the 'Trident' decisions on Burma made it necessary to lose no time in settling on the new commanders and command structure in India. Churchill had not yet completely reconciled himself to Wavell as Viceroy. He signalled the War Cabinet on 29 May, suggesting that Wavell could go to Australia as Governor-General. The War Cabinet's reply pointed out that to send a distinguished British field-marshal to Australia might upset the touchy Douglas MacArthur.[14] Since no British political figure of stature would go to India, and since he had to be let down gently, Wavell therefore became Viceroy. General Sir Claude J. E. Auchinleck was named to replace him as commander-in-chief. Unemployed since his removal by Churchill from the Middle East command the previous August, he had previously been considered for an Indian governorship, since the Prime Minister had lost confidence in him as a commander.[15] But Auchinleck was an Indian Army officer, and Brooke had pointed out to Churchill during 'Trident' that only Indian Army officers could get the best out of Indian troops.[16] Auchinleck would, in any case, only control operations in Burma as an interim measure because Churchill was determined to change machinery as well as men.

The principle was clear from the outset: the conduct of current operations in Burma and planning for the future, together with the administrative and constitutional responsibilities that

fell to the commander-in-chief, India, were far too heavy a
burden for any one man. According to a 26 May memorandum
by Attlee, presiding over the Defence Committee in Churchill's
absence, the Prime Minister initially considered the creation of a
new command structure on the Cairo model, where the three
commanders-in-chief formed a trinity of equals, with a Minister
of State, representing the War Cabinet, thrown in.[17] This
arrangement, the natural outgrowth of the British 'defence by
committee' system, was not really suitable to an allied command,
which South-East Asia would clearly have to be. On 27 May,
Amery submitted a paper to the Defence Committee proposing
an arrangement, based on Wavell's ABDA command or Eisenhower's allied headquarters in North Africa, which would take
over responsibility for operations against Japan from India.[18]
When the Prime Minister returned to Britain early in June,
arrangements along these lines were quickly agreed and, when
Wavell's new appointment was announced, together with Auchinleck's, on 18 June, the creation of a new South-East Asia
Command, to take over responsibility for operations from India
Command, was also promised. But, perhaps because of the Prime
Minister's preoccupation with other things, nothing was actually
done to set it up or name the new supreme commander, although
Amery, who was a keen supporter of the idea, had already suggested the Chief of Combined Operations, Vice-Admiral Lord
Louis Mountbatten, for the post.[19] The implementation of the
decisions taken at 'Trident' thus fell to Auchinleck, a state of
affairs that rapidly increased the Prime Minister's already considerable irritation with India Command.

Auchinleck had shown himself, during his year in the Middle
East, to be a very cautious commander when it came to making
forecasts. This trait had contributed powerfully to Churchill's
disenchantment with him, although in the field Auchinleck had
proved bold and cool, saving 'Crusader' in November 1941 and
checkmating Rommel the following July. When he became the
Indian Army's last, and perhaps its greatest, commander-in-chief
on 20 June 1943 he faced an array of difficulties that made
caution mandatory. The Indian Army, in the aftermath of the
Arakan fiasco, had to be nursed back to health and battleworthi-
ness. Moreover, two devastating calamities hit eastern India and
Assam, the base for operations into Burma, just as Auchinleck

assumed the responsibility for those operations. At least a million people died in the Bengal famine of 1943, itself a product of bad harvests, war-time dislocations within India, and the worldwide shipping crisis which cramped all allied affairs. Wavell, taking over as Viceroy, had to use the army to supplement the civil administration of the province which was collapsing under the combined weight of war, famine, and a lack of drive fortunately rare in the history of the Indian Civil Service. When the monsoon broke the situation got worse. Heavier than usual, the rains washed away bridges and roadbeds, severely disrupting communications in eastern India. Deliveries by rail to Calcutta were down by half. The possibility of carrying out the 'Trident' decisions in the face of all this was very slim, and, characteristically, Auchinleck lost no time in saying so. On 2 July he sent an appreciation home that made clear the problems involved in fulfilling the 'Trident' mandate in north Burma. The country would have to be cleared as far south as Mandalay, he pointed out, if the Ledo Road and the old Burma Road were to be not only joined but made secure. Administrative problems, however, would prevent this being done in one dry season, so that the operation would not be complete until 1944-45. Turning to the amphibious operations approved at 'Trident', Auchinleck asked for larger resources, because morale in India and its army required a clear success in the first operation of this sort mounted from the Indian base. Larger resources for 'Bullfrog' – Akyab's new designation – meant, however, that the companion operation to capture Ramree would also have to be put off until after the 1944 monsoon. This assessment, which meant no road to China open until 1945 at the earliest, made unpleasant reading in London. The commander-in-chief administered a second dose three weeks later in a supplementary appreciation stressing the problems of mounting 'Bullfrog' and questioning the necessity for assaulting Ramree.[20] With a convalescent army and railways disappearing in monsoon mud, there was not much else Auchinleck could have cabled home, but it produced an explosion from the Prime Minister.

The Joint Planning Staff had commented that, despite Auchinleck's reservations, the 'Trident' decisions had to be carried out 'in the interests of Anglo-American cooperation if nothing else.'[21] The Prime Minister, who knew better than anyone the impact that delays in clearing Burma might have on those relations, dictated an angry minute on 26 July.

> Since General Auchinleck has given his mind to this problem, the impulse has been to magnify the difficulties, to demand even larger forces and to prescribe far longer delays . . . It also shows how vital and urgent is the appointment of a young competent soldier, well trained in war, to become Supreme Commander and to re-examine the whole problem of the war on this front so as to infuse vigour and audacity into the operation. The kind of paper we have received from General Auchinleck would rightly excite the deepest suspicions in the United States that we are only playing and dawdling with the war in this theatre.[22]

Two days later he returned to the same point at a Defence Committee meeting. The tempo of operations proposed by Auchinleck would embarrass the British at the next Anglo-American summit: 'we should be criticized by the Americans for our lack of enterprise and drive'. To restore the appearance of dynamism, he proposed to increase the airlift and use an ex-panded Long Range Penetration force in Burma. However, he added, 'in view of the small scale of our operations on the Assam frontier and the bleak prospects at Akyab and Ramree, he would like to put across to the Americans a bold concept for the sum-mer of 1944, on the lines of the operation against Sumatra.' The Prime Minister's heart belonged to this operation, known as 'Culverin'. He did not want a full-scale campaign in Burma. His real complaint with Auchinleck was that he was not proposing something that would combine activity in Burma with avoidance of major operations there. Brooke pointed out to Churchill that 'Culverin' was not an end in itself but merely the first step on the way back to Singapore, but opening *that* road would require forces that would only be available after the defeat of Germany (which was now estimated to occur in March 1945). Wavell, who was present for this discussion, added that, while he was out of touch, he felt that completely bypassing Burma was the soundest idea. In the end the Committee decided that the 'Trident' deci-sions ought to be reviewed, since nothing could be done anyway till 1944 (thus accepting Auchinleck's arguments), and that the Americans should be asked to consider the advantages of by-passing Burma.[23] In view of what had happened at 'Trident' both these conclusions seem unrealistic. The Americans had made a bargain: further Mediterranean operations in return for a firm date for 'Overlord' and a set of agreements on Burma. Everything that had happened since 'Arcadia' should have told the British that the legalistic cast of the American official mind would take a dim view indeed of what the British were now proposing to do. Churchill's remarks about the value of LRP operations indicated the solution which was taking shape in his mind to the problem of satisfying the Americans while avoiding a major campaign in Burma, but on 28 July his attention and that of the Defence Committee was really on the Mediterranean and on Burma only as it might affect the British capacity to influence developments there.

In a minute to the Chiefs of Staff late in July, in which he sketched out his grand design for the defeat of Japan, Churchill remarked, almost complacently, that 'the Americans will be gratified at the interest we are taking in the Japanese war and at our earnest preparations to undertake it, *and the introduction of this topic as a major issue at "QUADRANT" will perhaps make other, nearer decisions more easy.*'[24] Behind this lay the vistas opening up in the Mediterranean. Sicily was successfully invaded on 10 July; Rome bombed on the 19th. The Fascist Grand Council revolted against Mussolini on the 24th, and the following day he was arrested. The imminent collapse of Italy, opening up the southern flank of the Axis, was an opportunity too precious to lose. In this mood the Chiefs of Staff examined the plans proposed by Eisenhower's headquarters for the invasion of Italy. On the morning of 28 July, they froze all of that command's amphibious assets, including some earmarked at 'Trident' as drawing rights for Auchinleck. They felt that Eisenhower, most of whose forces were British or British controlled, should have the maximum flexibility at what might prove a moment of fleeting opportunity. Churchill was wholeheartedly behind them, although for slightly different reasons. In his struggle to maintain Anglo-American parity, the achievements of the largely British (although American-veneered) Mediterranean forces were, in his eyes, a vital asset. Visions of Rome danced in his head and he would not spoil them for what he stigmatized as a 'bleak Bull-frog'. The Defence Committee meeting later on the 28th approved the 'standstill order' issued that morning, and agreed that the Mediterranean opportunities were far more significant than the capture of Akyab. Two months after 'Trident', the British had virtually repudiated the agreements made there on the Far East. Nature had made them almost impossible administratively and Auchinleck had merely pointed this out. The British had then swung back, like a compass needle returning to north, to an amphibious strategy. They had also revealed, especially to suspicious American eyes, their real priorities by proposing 'Culverin', something no more immediately feasible than operations in Burma, and then unilaterally holding assault shipping and troop lift in the Mediterranean to pursue what many Americans thought of as a peculiarly British war. Against this background of cross purposes and rising irritation, the impasse that developed as British and American planners sought a combined strategy for the defeat of Japan is not surprising.

'At "Quadrant" we should raise the whole question of the war against Japan in an urgent form,' Churchill told the Chiefs of Staff late in July, in the minute referred to above.

> Obviously we should probably carry the war through Burma, Java and Sumatra, into the Malay Peninsula, while the United States undertook the mastery of various islands and the reconquest of the Philippines. We should probably also require to take Formosa in combination, and to establish landings and air power in China. If Russia comes in on our side, as is a 51–49 probability, the great air attack on Metropolitan Japan could be made from Russian and Chinese bases. How very convenient it would be to supplement or anticipate this by refueling stations provided by a number of 'HABBAKUKS'* prepared in Alaska or the Aleutians and towed into position in these very cold waters.[25]

'Habbakuks' apart, this scheme broadly defined the consensus that had been taking shape in British planning circles over the past six months. The problem was that it left politics, and the emotions that lay behind them, out of account. Churchill wanted a 'full and fair place' in the war against Japan for Britain, but suspicions about British motives, and the obvious ineffectiveness of British actions in that war so far, had bred a determination in the Americans to get what they felt was needed (and had been promised at 'Trident'). It was the Asian counterpart of Marshall's

---

*Self-propelled islands of artificial ice, or 'Pyecrete', envisioned as floating airfields – the brainchild of Dr R. Pye, a scientist on the staff of Mountbatten's Combined Operations Headquarters.

obsession with pinning the British to a firm date for 'Overlord'.
As long ago as May, Lieutenant-General Stanley Embick, one of
the War Department's more anglophobe planners, had warned
Marshall that if the British recaptured Singapore, they would rest
content, leaving the United States alone to finish the Japanese
war.[26] Everything that had happened since, especially the fate
of the 'Trident' decisions culminating in the unilateral British
standstill order, reinforced such doubts. On 7 August the Joint
Staff Mission in Washington cabled the Chiefs of Staff a warning: 'There is an increasing feeling with the US Chiefs that we
do not mean business in Burma, and have never meant business
in Burma.'[27] A document produced the same day by the Joint
Planning Staff could well have been cited by the Americans as
documentary proof of their fears.

> An overland advance in Burma from the North and West with
> Rangoon as the final objective is likely to be a protracted, costly
> and difficult operation, in which most of the best cards will be in
> the enemy's hands. We do not recommend it.[28]

What they did recommend, if Burma had to be cleared, was a
combined airborne and seaborne assault on Rangoon – which,
of course, everyone agreed could not be done until 1944-45. The
following day, as if by a mind-reading trick, the American Joint
Chiefs produced their response: 'The early increase in assistance
to China is of the utmost importance in keeping her in the war.
In addition to assisting China materially, our air efforts in China
will be furthered.' Since the British could not clear all Burma in
1943-44, the Joint Chiefs felt that their contribution that year
should take the form of reopening a land route by operations in
the north.[29] Deadlock was complete and, with sharpened tempers, especially in Washington, potentially more dangerous than
the situation before 'Trident'.

Churchill was again on his way to Quebec when these docu-
ments were produced. The *Queen Mary* left the Clyde for Halifax
on 5 August. 'Quadrant' was the Prime Minister's last chance to
square the circle – to appease the Americans while avoiding the
thraldom of Burma. It was also the midway point in the most
conference-strewn year of the wartime alliance. The frequency
with which the principals met was a function, among other
things, of a shift in the internal power balance of the 'Grand

Alliance'. In 1942 it had clearly been the British who had made the running. In spite of the disasters that beset them in every theatre until the autumn (and long after that in Burma), they imposed their pattern on the war. British mobilization of men and resources was nearing its peak, and far more British and British-controlled forces were in contact with the enemy than American. Furthermore, the British had superior organization at the top, a clear idea of what they wanted to do – against Germany at least – and a leader of great force and ability. American potential, however, was enormous, and disorganization at the centre, while never likely to be entirely tidied up under Roosevelt, was rapidly being reduced to manageable proportions. A clear consciousness of the disparity between their resources and those of the British, an abounding confidence based on that abundance, and the ancient ambivalence of Americans confronted with the descendants of those mythical oppressors who stalked the pages of their elementary school primers, all combined to produce rising irritation at British dominance over alliance strategy. Field-Marshal Sir John Dill, head of the Joint Staff Mission in Washington, had cautioned Brooke in the autumn of 1942: 'We have in fact imposed our strategy upon them and they are very conscious of it.'[30] But it was not until the 1943 round of conferences, beginning with Casablanca, that British caution, born of painful experience and limited resources, began to encounter stiffer and stiffer opposition from the Americans. The British had to run harder and harder just to keep from falling too far behind. Decisions affecting the war against Japan are a good barometer of this development, because the British tended to give way there first in order to protect their more important Mediterranean schemes. At Casablanca, Churchill agreed to a plan of campaign in Burma 'largely as a concession to United States opinion'. At 'Trident', three months later, there was little pretence of gracious concession. Roosevelt imposed a programme nearly the opposite of what the British had come prepared to advocate. Churchill had, however, kept his Mediterranean options open. It was a further move in his struggle to maintain the British position in the alliance, preserve strategic flexibility in Europe, and satisfy the Americans over Burma, that now brought Orde Wingate on board the *Queen Mary* for the voyage to Canada.

Since emerging from Burma, Wingate had written a report on Chindit I, in which he staked out wide claims for a vastly expanded LRP force, and then had a serious misunderstanding with army headquarters in Delhi over the printing and circulation of that report. A copy reached Amery, however, in mid-July and he saw to it that it came to Churchill's attention.[31] This, together with the publicity attaching to the one successful feat of arms on what an official historian was later to call 'these least glorious of British battlefields'[32], brought Wingate forcefully to the Prime Minister's notice at precisely the moment when Auchinleck's cautious approach to implementing the 'Trident' decisions brought the Prime Minister to the end of his always limited patience with the Indian military authorities. Two days after Auchinleck's second gloomy appreciation an angry minute went to the Chiefs of Staff. Dismissing the efforts of the preceding eighteen months as a 'welter of lassitude and inefficiency', Churchill demanded a radical change in India that would make Lieutenant-General Sir Oliver Leese, then commanding Montgomery's XXX Corps in Sicily, theatre commander, with Wingate in control of operations in Burma. He brushed aside the latter's lack of seniority and ordered him brought home for consultations.[33] Wingate left India within a few days and reached London literally on the eve of the Prime Minister's departure. After a meeting with Brook and a brief interview at 10 Downing Street, Wingate was added to Churchill's party, which already included another symbol of heroic British martial endeavour in the shape of Wing-Commander Guy Gibson, VC, the leader of the 'Dam Busters'.

The Prime Minister, it is true, always was susceptible to the romantic appeal of glamorous military figures, and Wingate, fresh, or nearly so, from the Burmese jungles certainly fitted this description. But Churchill's decision to bring him home from India, and take him on to 'Quadrant', was due less to impulse and emotion, or to memories of Wingate's distant relative, T. E. Lawrence, than to the opportunity Wingate seemed to offer to solve, at a stroke, three interlocking problems: American doubts about British willingness to take seriously the clearing of Burma; British doubts about the wisdom of doing so in the way the Americans wished; and the desire shared by Prime Minister and his advisers to shape a British amphibious strategy for the war against Japan. At a meeting of the Chiefs of Staff on board ship, Churchill pointed out that by making use of LRP groups, north Burma could be cleared and the road to China completed. Restoration of communications with China would satisfy the Americans, reconcile them to the virtual abandonment of the 'Trident' decisions, and save resources for 'Culverin', now firmly settled as the centrepiece of the Prime Minister's own strategic design.[34] On 7 August he minuted that Wingate's report should be circulated to the American Chiefs of Staff and Wingate himself allowed to expound his plans to them 'and thus convince them that we mean business in this sector of the South-East Asia Front.'[35] The next day Wingate presented his plans to the British Chiefs of Staff. By this time, in the favourable atmosphere he had found since his return to England, those ideas had become rather grandiose. For 1943-44, three LRP groups, backed by three more to replace them after twelve weeks, would converge from China and Assam on north Burma, disrupt Japanese communications, and open the way for an advance by British and Chinese 'main forces'. This process would be repeated in 1944-45, clearing the rest of Burma and moving on into Thailand and Indochina. To accomplish all this, Wingate would need two things: supply aircraft and 'a machine for turning out LRPGs at a steady and increasing rate.'[36] The first demand meant that someone would have to find a very large number of transport aircraft somewhere – there was one operational RAF squadron in India equipped with American-built Dakotas (Douglas C-47s – the best aircraft for supply-dropping), and the British were completely dependent on the Americans for further aircraft of this type, having eschewed building transports in 1940 in favour of combat aircraft.* The second was a thinly disguised request for control of the army in India, for only by taking over and cannibalizing its formations could Wingate quickly get his initial force of six groups (roughly equivalent to a corps) and the much larger forces needed for his 1944-45 programme. Beyond this, there were serious questions of feasibility and the relation of means to ends that ought to have been raised about Wingate's proposals. The sequel to his presentation was, however, very

---

*There were, of course, a large number of transport aircraft based in India, but they belonged to the American ferry command that flew the Hump airlift, and were controlled directly from Washington.

revealing. The Chiefs of Staff turned Wingate's ideas over to the Joint Planners who, properly cautious, proposed to seek Auchinleck's views. They were quickly brought up short by their masters, who redrafted the message so as to make it unmistakably clear to the commander-in-chief that Wingate's proposals had been adopted and that he was being asked only about their implementation.[87]

The decision 'to make the maximum possible use of long range penetration groups in Burma'[88] is decidedly curious. After one verbal briefing by a hitherto obscure gunner, not noted for his polish or diplomatic skills (he struck one member of Churchill's staff as having a 'fanatical light in his eye', and thinking his opponents 'knaves or fools'[89]), the Chiefs of Staff adopted a decidedly unorthodox strategy for clearing north Burma, without seeking any estimate of what it would cost in manpower and disruption in India, and in spite of the glaring fact that the British did not have the resources in transport aircraft to implement it. Indeed, the Chiefs of Staff went out of their way not to have the problems pointed out to them. The explanation for this rather odd procedure seems to lie in the Prime Minister's determination to spring a dazzling British initiative on the Americans. He had told the Chiefs of Staff at the beginning of the voyage that he insisted on 'positive proposals for attacking the enemy, and proving our zeal in this theatre of war, which by its failures and sluggishness is in a measure under reasonable reproach.'[40] Auchinleck could offer only intractable reality; Wingate offered a beguiling vision with, perhaps, more than a dash of fantasy, but one that met the political needs of the hour. Since Wingate's operations were to serve an American aim, the British may well have felt that the Americans could reduce the fantasy element by providing the necessary resources. In any case, when the *Queen Mary* docked at Halifax, the British had a new policy to replace the defunct 'Trident' decisions for Burma: Wingate.

One other matter agitated the Prime Minister as he sailed westward – a new theatre commander for South-East Asia. Leese, if he was ever a serious possibility, dropped out early, which was just as well since his range of abilities stopped well short of the characteristics needed. A more serious contender was Air Chief Marshal Sir W. Sholto Douglas, then commanding the RAF in the Middle East. Churchill had, Ismay recalled six years later, 'practically decided on Sholto Douglas, when the Americans represented that he would not be acceptable to them, as he had been known to make adverse comments on Americans as a whole, and the American Air Force in particular . . .' Ismay added that 'all the names submitted by the Chiefs of Staff were very ordinary.'[41] Since these names included Air Chief Marshal Sir Arthur Tedder, and Admiral Sir Andrew B. Cunningham, Ismay's characterization is unusual. But both Cunningham and Tedder were deeply involved in the Mediterranean. One member of Churchill's staff, invited to propose names, suggested Lieutenant-General Sir George Giffard, who had recently taken over from Irwin, only to be told by the Prime Minister that Mountbatten was his choice.[42] Amery had, of course, already put his name forward and Ismay later wrote to Churchill, 'I believe your mind was working in the direction of Mountbatten all the time . . .'[43] Mountbatten, young, charming, and open-minded (he was Dr Pye's sponsor), known to, and approved by, Roosevelt and the American Chiefs of Staff, familiar with the central war direction in London, was an inspired choice.

The British thus had new faces and new policies to present at Quebec. It only remained to sell them to the Americans. At a meeting on the *Queen Mary*, the Chiefs of Staff had decided not to put before the Americans a new programme of operations from India into Burma, but merely to report the 'progress' made in implementing the 'Trident' decisions in the light of the 'new facts' that had since emerged: the disruption of communications in eastern India by the monsoon, and the emergence of Wingate.[44] Clearly, the British hoped this would lead to an agreement on future operations in Burma that was within the limits of what they believed to be both feasible and desirable. They then hoped to pass on to the larger question of British participation in the final defeat of Japan. British planners firmly believed the British contribution should be an amphibious blow at northern Sumatra, opening the way for the reconquest of Singapore, although they recognized that the year's delay would not be welcome to the Americans, and the Chiefs of Staff had accepted that it would be necessary to carry on in Burma in some way, if only for the sake of alliance solidarity. In any case they did not expect to be able to do much in South-East Asia until after the defeat of Germany released British resources from Europe.

Churchill, however, wanted to leave Burma to Wingate and get on with 'Culverin'. The Prime Minister also planned to raise the question of the Royal Navy's participation in the Pacific war, a symbolic point of great importance to him.

Although operations in Burma are the focus of the discussion here, it must not be forgotten that the principal item on the agenda at Quebec was the continuing Anglo-American argument over the relationship between the Mediterranean and the invasion of North-West Europe. The British were again reasonably successful in protecting their interests in the Mediterranean, although the confrontation between the British and American Chiefs of Staff on 16 August was the most tense yet to occur, and was only resolved when the room was cleared of all save the Chiefs themselves. The curiously inconclusive nature of much of the discussions on Burma and the Pacific probably owes a great deal to the preoccupation of the principals with European matters and an unwillingness to disturb hard-won amity over them by a clash over what was for both a secondary matter. Brooke produced Wingate, whose presentation made a considerable impression on the Americans, especially on General Marshall. In the final report of the Combined Chiefs of Staff to the President and Prime Minister on 25 August, land operations in north Burma to open communications with China during the impending dry season, figured once again. On the larger matter of ending the Japanese war, the final report was rather nebulous, since the British and American planners simply could not agree.

During the months between 'Trident' and 'Quadrant' British and American planners had exchanged ideas, seeking an 'agreed strategic concept' for the defeat of Japan. They kept coming up against Burma and the road to China. The British planners wanted to leave Burma to Wingate and China to the airlift, and go for Sumatra and Singapore, despite the fact that this would mean no major operations until 1944-45. The Americans, however, wanted Burma completely cleared during the 1943-44 and 1944-45 dry seasons, before any assault on Malaya was mounted. At bottom, differing attitudes about the purpose of the British war effort in the east prevented agreement. The Americans wanted a supply line to China, as much in the interest of an air offensive against Japan as of Chiang's army by this time, and were relatively indifferent to the recovery of Singapore by the

British, whether or not it was strategically sound. Marshall agreed at 'Quadrant' that opening the Malacca Straits and the South China Sea were an alternative to reopening the Burma Road, but still argued for clearing Burma first.[45] The British, on the other hand, not only believed an amphibious strategy to be correct, but also were attracted by the recovery by imperial arms of the 'fortress' whose loss was the greatest military calamity their empire had ever suffered. The British position was summarized in a paper submitted to the Combined Chiefs on 18 August, the day after the European differences had finally been composed.

> The British Planners feel strongly that the question of whether or not China remains in the war will not be decided by the choice between Course B (the prior capture of Burma) and Course C (the prior capture of Singapore) since China's darkest hours will be in the early half of 1944, before Germany is defeated. Thereafter, the obvious weight of the United Nations offensive against Japan in general and the prospect of an early opening of the sea route in particular will do more to sustain morale than the arrival of limited additional material through Burma, always provided supply by the air route continues at the maximum.
>
> The British Planners feel strongly that the recapture of Southern Burma and Rangoon would be a small strategic gain for the expenditure of great effort. At best it would: (a) produce limited pressure on Japanese land and air forces for two dry seasons with little attrition during the intervening wet season, (b) open the Burma road. As this cannot in any case be in full operation before some time in 1946, whether we go for Rangoon or Singapore first, the results are long term. In the unlikely event of the Japanese in the meantime occupying Kunming, all our efforts in Burma would be nullified.
>
> On the other hand, the British Planners feel that the recapture of Singapore before Rangoon is a full and correct application of sea and air power. *It will electrify the eastern world* and have an immense psychological effect on the Japanese. It will . . . in fact flank and undermine the whole Japanese defense structure in Southeast Asia.[46]

The use of Wingate's LRP groups in fact represented the only area of the war against Japan in South-East Asia where there was complete agreement between the allies at Quebec, and the final report reflected this. 'We have found it impracticable during "Quadrant" to arrive at all the necessary decisions for operations against Japan in 1943-44,' read the preamble to the section on specific operations in the Pacific and South-East Asia. The 'main effort' in the latter was to be the opening of land communications with China, and agreement on this objective was only made possible by mutual acceptance of Wingate's as yet unproven ideas. The British also, as a consequence, accepted American aid to improve the Assam line of communications that had to sustain both the airlift and Wingate. For the rest, agreement was reached that Japan should be defeated within a year of Germany's demise. To wait until 1947-48 might lead to a compromise peace through waning public willingness to go on – something that was already worrying some members of Churchill's government. The new South-East Asia Command was ordered to prepare an amphibious operation of the size originally contemplated for Akyab and Ramree, but its objective was again left open – a success for Churchill who was set upon turning it into 'Culverin'. In the list of 'studies' ordered for future operations, the various objectives considered by British planners – northern Sumatra, Moulmein, the Kra Isthmus leading on to Bangkok, and a direct assault on Singapore via the Malacca Straits – all appeared, together with the American favourites, Akyab, Ramree, and a drive southward towards Rangoon from northern Burma during the 1944-45 dry season. In short everything except expanded Chindit operations and the airlift – both of which served essentially American ends – was left for future resolution.[47]

The pressure of other business and desire to avoid further confrontation partially explains this, as does the fact that the Americans got what they wanted. But it is also true that the decision actually to establish the South-East Asia Command (SEAC) forecast at 'Trident', and name a commander, meant that some latitude had to be left for SEAC to study the problem and formulate recommendations. The creation of SEAC, like agreement on Wingate, came remarkably easily – another case of the impact of personality perhaps – although working out the details again brought mutual suspicions to the surface. Setting up the new command, and separating it from GHQ, India, which would remain, however, in control of training and the administration of the Indian base, had already been agreed. Mountbatten proved an acceptable candidate to the Americans. When Churchill broached the idea to him, he asked for a day to consider, somewhat to the Prime Minister's surprise. Coming into Ismay's room he told him of the offer and remarked 'I feel as though I had been pole-axed.' Mountbatten's spasm of concern was soon vanquished by his customary self-confidence and the assurance that he would have American as well as British backing. In any case he had realized for some time that the work of Combined Operations Headquarters would increasingly be overshadowed by the 'Overlord' structure and was looking for something new to absorb his very remarkable combination of talent and energy.[48] But if the Supreme Commander's appointment was easily handled, the command structure over which he was to preside gave no end of trouble.

To begin with there was Stilwell. By this time the British had had rather more than enough of him (as had Chiang, for different reasons). Following precedents established by ABDA and Eisenhower's headquarters, a supreme commander from one country was balanced by a deputy from the other. Stilwell was the obvious candidate and, much as the British might have wished for nearly any other American, Marshall represented that Stilwell was essential because his appointment would allow the claim to be made that all American forces in SEAC were there primarily to aid China.[49] It is also true that since Stilwell had become identified in American eyes with support for China and criticism of the British, passing him over might have been politically embarrassing. So Mountbatten was saddled with Stilwell, who still held his multiplicity of appointments, one of which, as Chiang's Chief of Staff, was quite independent of SEAC.

That this astonishing arrangement – it was as if Brooke had been named as Eisenhower's deputy and an army commander for 'Overlord' while remaining CIGS – should have been allowed to continue for another year is eloquent testimony to the American belief that the British would not do what they wished in Burma unless they had the leverage to force the British to do so. The British Chiefs of Staff were designated as the channel through which Mountbatten would report to the Combined Chiefs, thus preserving appearances (although Stilwell could always find in one of his appointments justification for dealing directly with Washington). However, the Joint Chiefs reserved to themselves control of all American aircraft in SEAC, most of which were working the airlift.[50] That reservation meant that the Americans would soon control the majority of Mountbatten's transport aircraft, a point that gave them further leverage. The structure of SEAC masked incompatible aims and unresolved disagreements – real potential for chaos in command.

In the aftermath of 'Quadrant' Churchill visited Washington – and so did Wingate. Churchill's eyes were on the rapidly developing Italian situation, but, with the easing of pressure in the Mediterranean, he took the opportunity of offering British ships for the Pacific, only to be told by Admiral Ernest J. King, the anglophobe Chief of Naval Operations, that while welcome they were not really needed.[51] At the same time Wingate and Mountbatten were conferring with American service leaders. General Arnold promised Wingate an air task force to work with the Chindits, and Marshall made it clear that these additional resources were being sent solely to make Wingate's plans possible and would be removed if those operations – like the 'Trident' operations – were pared down or cancelled.[52] At this point the consequences of selling Wingate so successfully to the Americans began to be apparent. Prior to 'Quadrant', American leverage on the British in South-East Asia grew out of the British need for American support elsewhere. Now the Americans had been persuaded not only to accept a strategy – clearing north Burma by LRP operations – but to make it possible by a heavy commitment of material. The British henceforth would have to operate in north Burma or face not only the political consequences of American irritation, but the loss of American resources, which could not be made good. The British had escaped from 'Anakim' and its variants only by nailing themselves to the one operation they disliked most – clearing north Burma for American roadbuilders.

The Prime Minister was not yet very concerned by all this. He had preserved on paper the amphibious possibilities that were nearest his heart, and all the evidence indicates that he felt he had solved the conundrum of Burma and could now concentrate on 'Culverin'. Back in London on 28 September, he presided over a meeting of the Defence Committee – only the second one incidentally to discuss the Far East during 1943 – at which he made the direction of his thinking plain.

The Prime Minister said that he preferred an operation against the northern tip of Sumatra. He felt that what was required in the Indian Ocean was an 'amphibious circus'. The improvement of our position in the Mediterranean, which would continue as we captured ports such as Naples would free considerable resources for operations in other theatres. He felt that the requirements of Culverin as now estimated, were excessive. Whilst he did not insist that an operation should be undertaken in March, since he was doubtful if the assault forces could be trained by that date, he felt very strongly that an operation such as First Culverin should be undertaken in the spring of 1944; its control must be British, and we should not send any ships to the Pacific if this would prejudice Culverin.[53]

Of course King had already rebuffed Churchill's attempt to introduce a symbolic British presence in the Pacific, but the remark about British control is a pointer toward one of Churchill's motives: the restoration, by British arms, of British prestige in an area where it had been so badly battered. In a paper on India a week later he declared roundly: 'We shall certainly not be in a worse position to deal with the constitutional position in India after we have beaten Germany and Japan and have revived the prestige of our arms in Burma and Malaya . . . Victory is the best foundation for great constitutional departures.'[54] On 10 October he initialled Wavell's directive as Viceroy, instructing him to see that India was 'a safe and fertile base from which the British and American offensive can be launched in 1944.'[55] The offensive he had in mind appeared in Mountbatten's directive, issued on Trafalgar Day (21 October). 'You will utilize to the full the advantages of seapower' the new supreme commander was told, 'you will proceed to form . . . a Combined Striking Force or Circus which will be available as the foundation of whatever amphibious descent is eventually chosen.' Compared to this the instruction to 'maintain and broaden our contacts with China' by air and ground sounds rather tepid.[56] Yet Burma was not to be so lightly dismissed. In addition to European pressures and American wishes, a chain of events had already begun, in India and in various Japanese headquarters, that was rapidly to make unreal the discussions in London about an amphibious strategy. The first link in that chain was the transformation of the Indian Army – even as Churchill prepared to displace it as the backbone of the imperial war effort in the east.

(ii)

If morale in the Indian Army was at a low ebb after the Arakan offensive, it was matched by the low opinion in which the Prime Minister held it. Aboard the *Queen Mary*, on the way to 'Trident', he treated Wavell to a tirade in which he dug into his historical memory and accumulated prejudices to denounce the Indian Army for various failings reaching all the way back to the Mutiny.[57] Behind this rather petulant outburst lay an accumulation of anxiety in London about the political reliability of the swollen and much battered Indian Army. In a paper for the War Cabinet on India's war effort some months earlier, Amery had defended the Indian Army vigorously, but warned that recruiting for further expansion from the 'martial classes' was at an end.[58] On 10 May, in the aftermath of the Arakan fiasco, he wrote another paper, this time on morale in the Indian Army.

> The prewar Indian Army was, of course, a mercenary army in so far as the men were volunteers, seeking a means of livelihood, not conscripts: but it was a professional army of men who chose the profession of arms as good in itself and were imbued, as part of their professional instinct, with a devotion to their regiment and to the Sirkar. A considerable proportion of the present army are mercenary in a lower sense; they are in it for what they can get and not actuated, at any rate when they join, by devotion to a distant throne or by any sentiment of loyalty to 'the colours' or by an instinctive 'esprit de corps' or by hatred of the enemy.

Amery also dilated upon the disturbing effect of discussions about India's political future: 'Proposals for changes in the political constitution of India and consequent uncertainty regarding the position of the Indian Army under any new constitution has raised, even in the minds of pre-war soldiers, doubts whether the British Raj is worth serving for anything but what it pays in cash and kind.'[59] This, together with Amery's preceding papers, seems to have convinced Churchill – who was predisposed to believe it in any case – that the problem with the Indian Army was simple: too many non-martial class recruits and too much politics, although a paper circulated on 17 May should have modified the picture. An extract of a letter from GHQ, India, written at the end of February, it pointed out that what really concerned rank and file soldiers was the effect of India's rampant inflation upon their families.[60] It is also odd that nobody in London, especially the Prime Minister, seems to have grasped that if the Indian Army was unreliable, it would have shown itself so during the August 1942 Congress Revolt, when the disorders had to be suppressed largely by Indian troops. (The Indian Army's only mutinous outbreak of the war in fact occurred in 1940 when two-thirds of a Sikh squadron of the Central India Horse refused to go aboard ship at Bombay.[61]) But the Prime Minister's eyes were henceforth firmly fixed on the size of the Indian Army and its class composition.

Churchill read Amery's paper on the way to 'Trident' – it may have fuelled his outburst to Wavell. At any rate he fired off a telegram to the Secretary of State: 'I am of opinion that not only should all expansion be stopped but that there should be a substantial reduction in the existing numbers, aimed at quality rather than quantity.' Waspishly he added, 'we ought to have heard all about this a good deal earlier.'[62] In fact, warnings of the consequences of over-expansion had been ample, but the War Cabinet, under Churchill's impulsion, had *then* wanted the largest possible Indian Army, primarily for the Middle East. The Prime Minister's new tack was quickly reflected by the Chiefs of Staff, who, on 18 May, asked Wavell for his views on a reduction in the size of the Indian Army. Wavell agreed that further expansion was unwise, but wanted to postpone any reductions pending, among other things, the findings of a committee he had set up to examine the state of the Indian Army's infantry.[63] Nonetheless, on Churchill's initiative, the War Cabinet, presided over by Attlee, agreed on 20 May to reduce the Indian Army's target figure to fifteen infantry and two armoured divisions, as well as to monitor Indian economic conditions in case pay rises became necessary.[64] By 18 June, Attlee had become convinced that they were, and Churchill readily agreed, although giving his assent his own particular twist. 'I entirely agree with the Deputy Prime Minister that the pay of the Indian Army should be increased. Broadly speaking, I should make a 25 percent reduction in the numbers and spread the saving over the pay of the rest.' 'You had better get a move on about the Indian

Army,' he added, 'which may otherwise prove to be a very great danger and encumbrance.'[65] Amery took his time replying to this, and when he did, on 3 August, it was to point out that the target figure for the Indian Army had already been reduced twice, once by the War Cabinet's decision in May, and a second time by the decision taken in India to convert two infantry divisions into training formations. He added that 1.2 million of the Indian Army's ration strength of 2 million were in fact 'ancillary troops' badly needed, not only in India itself but in the Middle East and in Persia and Iraq Command. 'In addition to this to make sweeping reductions in strengths might have the most unfortunate repercussions on morale . . . and . . . create an atmosphere of distrust . . . difficult to justify to our allies,' Amery concluded, no doubt with the impending 'Quadrant' meeting in mind.[66] The Prime Minister found himself replying to Amery from mid-ocean again, and his reply is a sad revelation of how impervious Churchill was to reasoned argument on this subject. 'I am increasingly concerned at the size of the Indian native army . . . It bears no relation to the splendid old time Indian units on which we have relied both overseas and in India. In my view, further reductions beside the two divisions are indispensable . . . the units preserved . . . should be formed of the best men and the martial races . . .'[67] The Prime Minister never wearied of the theme. In his 6 October paper on Indian policy he gave as one of his reasons for opposing political change during the war that 'we have an enormously swollen Indian Army of a very much lower quality than we have ever had before,' and Wavell's directive as Viceroy four days later echoed this: 'beware above all things lest the achievement of victory . . . should be retarded by undue concentration on political issues . . .'[68] The belief that the Indian Army was full of unsuitable material, low in morale and of little offensive value, was reinforced by the opinions of General Irwin, back in England after his relief from command in India. In September he met Mountbatten and the latter's Chief of Staff, Lieutenant-General Sir Henry Pownall, and told them (and presumably anyone else who was willing to listen) that the Indian Army and the British troops in India were in such poor shape that at least two years would be needed before they would be ready for battle.[69] Wingate, whose stock was higher than Irwin's, held an equally low opinion of the Indian Army.

The irony in all this is that concern in London was at its most intense when the problems had either passed or were passing. The supposed political unreliability of the Indian Army was a phantasm of Churchill's own creation. Neither Congress rioters, inflation, the Bengal famine, nor Subhas Chandra Bose's Japanese-sponsored Indian National Army affected the Indian Army's loyalty. Weaknesses due to over-rapid expansion, lack of training and equipment, and preparation for the wrong war were certainly real enough. But by May 1943 the Indian Army was beginning to grapple with these problems as well. Two actions by Wavell, in his last days as commander-in-chief, were of great importance. By telegram from Washington on 16 May, he ordered his deputy, General Sir Alan Hartley, to establish a committee to examine and report on the state of British and Indian infantry in India Command. Sitting from 1-14 June, the committee quickly came up with sound, if obvious, recommendations: the infantry must henceforth receive the best recruits, NCOs and officers; they must all be better trained individually and collectively; 'milking' of formations with the accompanying dispatch of raw recruits into combat must end; and two training divisions were needed to prepare men from depots and training centres for combat.[70] One of these recommendations had already been anticipated by the decision in London to end further expansion, and even to reduce the Indian Army somewhat. The rest were within the power of India command to implement. On 19 June, Hartley cabled London that recruits would now spend an extra month in training centres and two months with training formations. To provide the latter, two Indian divisions were being converted into training units. This would also have another benefit, Hartley pointed out. 'It has become evident that the flow of pre-war classes through infantry training centres is not sufficient to maintain the number of Indian Infantry Bns. of those classes now in the Army. This fact necessitates the withdrawal from the order of battle of Infantry to the equivalent of approx. Two Divs. Reductions required by the needs of training and of maintenance are therefore closely linked and the same two Divisions will meet both needs.'[71] (Characteristically, when the Chiefs of Staff approved this on 29 July, they remarked that it would render the Indian Army safer from subversion.[72])

Responsibility for infantry training was also changed at the same time, a critically important matter if the new training scheme was to succeed. In the aftermath of the retreat from Burma in 1942, Wavell had created an Inspector of Infantry to tackle the problem of retraining the Indian Army to meet the Japanese. However, he had then filled the position with a very tired man, Major-General J. Bruce Scott, who had commanded the 1st Burma Division throughout the withdrawal. A capable officer, and certainly experienced in fighting the Japanese, he was unfortunately so worn out by the rigours of the campaign that he was not able to impart the necessary drive to the immense job of re-orienting the Indian Army's training from the desert to the jungle. In the aftermath of the Arakan disaster, Wavell, rather late in the day, had recognized this and, on 11 June 1943, replaced Bruce Scott with a more dynamic man, Major-General Reginald Savory, then commanding the 23rd Indian Division in Assam. As Inspector (changed after a few months to Director) of Infantry, Savory, with wide powers over training, organization, arms and equipment, played a critical role for the rest of the war. He kept in touch with changing tactical requirements by frequent visits to the front, and the programmes run by his two training divisions were tough and realistic. This was supplemented when the troops reached their divisions in Burma, by highly specialized training to suit the particular circumstances in which the division was fighting. The end result of the process was soldiers ready, in Savory's words, 'to go anywhere and fight anything'. A similar training programme was set up for British troops in India. In addition two schools for officers were established in India to teach the latest tactical doctrine for war in Burma, and to emphasize the necessity to close cooperation between all arms. The revolution in training wrought by the reorganization of June 1943 and the hard work of Savory and his subordinates were the foundations for Slim's great victories.[73]

When Auchinleck took over as commander-in-chief in late July, the renovation of the Indian Army was, therefore, already underway. Auchinleck saw that the pace did not slacken. The Intelligence School at Karachi (the location – one of the principal ports of embarkation for the Middle East – is significant) had concentrated largely, and incredibly, on the German and Italian Armies hitherto. Colonel G. A. Wards, a Japanese-speaking former military attaché in Tokyo, was brought in as Commandant, and the supply of relevantly trained intelligence officers quickly improved. Auchinleck also made changes in the welfare organizations and arrangements for the troops, as well as tackling vigorously the immense problem of malaria prevention and treatment, and seeing to the provision of a more varied diet of fresh foodstuffs. Obviously he did not do it all alone, but the impulsion was his, and the fact that much of this had not been put in hand before indicates that the change of commanders-in-chief was very timely. Of all these alterations, the medical improvements were not only the most striking but possibly the most important. New drugs, tighter discipline to ensure the troops actually took them, and DDT to destroy the sources of the disease produced dramatic results. The ratio of sick to wounded that stood at 120:1 in 1943 dropped to 20:1 in 1944 and to 6:1 by the end of the war. The malaria rate dropped, during intense operations, from 84 percent of the strength of Eastern Army in 1943 to one per thousand per day in Fourteenth Army in 1945. Without this reduction it is hard to see how Slim's great campaigns of 1944-45 could have been sustained.[74]

As the basics – training, health, and welfare – began to raise morale, changes in commanders and tactical thinking laid the foundation for a future in which defeat would not again depress it. The Arakan campaign not only brought Wavell's replacement by Auchinleck, but Irwin's removal from Eastern Army. He was replaced by Lieutenant-General Sir George Giffard, who had been one of the British Army's progressives in the bleak years between the wars, and had come from West Africa, where he had been GOC. A man totally lacking in charisma, he nonetheless, as Slim later said, 'understood the fundamentals of war – that soldiers must be trained before they can fight, fed before they can march, and relieved before they are worn out.'[75] This marked a great advance on the past. But the most important change was the emergence of Slim himself. At the end of the Arakan offensive, Irwin compounded his previous errors by trying to sack Slim, after Slim had saved what could be saved but in doing so had withdrawn farther than Irwin wished. This, fortunately, was aborted by Irwin's own supercession.[76] During the ensuing summer, Slim, still commanding XV Corps, mulling over the lessons of the retreat from Burma and the Arakan campaign, produced the formula that was to turn the tide. His ideas, his official biographer has written, 'were bold but simple.'

> They were devised to counter an enemy whose reaction, made instinctive by training, was to bypass or infiltrate. In countries where forces are small and areas vast positions can always be turned. If the defender (who may of course be the attacker unexpectedly thrown on the defensive), holds well-stocked pivots of manoeuvre on approaches to vital areas the enemy will be forced to attack, to establish lines of communication to his infiltrating or outflanking forces. The pivots must then stand firm, supplied if necessary by air, and when the supply line of the infiltrators has been cut they can be destroyed by reserves: then a counter-offensive can be launched.[77]

The structure of Indian Army divisions was also changing during the summer and autumn of 1943, producing a force more adapted to the warfare Slim envisioned. In the aftermath of the 1941-42 disasters in Malaya and Burma, a conference in Delhi came to the obvious conclusion that tables of organization and equipment drawn up with the Middle East in mind produced fatally clumsy, road-bound units. As a solution, two changes were proposed. The first was the creation of Indian light divisions, with fewer men and vehicles – the latter all four-wheel drive – and dependent largely on pack mule transport companies; the second, the reduction of the degree of mechanization in some divisions, transforming them into 'A & MT' (animal and motor transport) divisions without reducing their strength as was done with the light divisions. Two divisions were chosen for transformation into light divisions, and four became A & MT formations. Auchinleck took these changes a step further, in the direction of greater jungle mobility and the reduction of mechanical transport to the essential minimum, and that exclusively four-wheel drive (made possible, of course, by a greater supply of such vehicles, especially the ubiquitous, and invaluable, jeep). The ground organization to support air supply, improvised in 1942 and greatly improved as a result of the experience gained in Chindit I, was also expanding as more air supply companies of the Royal Indian Army Service Corps were raised.[78] Together, Slim's new ideas, the new army and new spirit that was emerging as a result of Auchinleck's efforts and Savory's training, and the appointment to key corps and divisional commands of men like

Scoones (IV Corps), Briggs (5th Indian Division), Messervy (7th Indian Division), Cowan (17th Indian Division), Gracey (20th Indian Division) and Roberts (23rd Indian Division), proven in battle, promised very different results in the 1943-44 campaigning season.

The arrival, in the midst of all this, of orders to enlarge Wingate's Special Force came as a very unwelcome surprise. After Chindit I, Wingate's original LRP formation (77th Indian Infantry Brigade) had been reformed and three additional battalions (one British and two Gurkha) had been drafted to form a second group (111th Indian Infantry Brigade). The mandate contained in the Chiefs of Staff signal of 14 August, making Wingate's earlier presentation to them official policy, ballooned this force into a substantial private army: a modified corps headquarters and the manpower equivalent of two full divisions would be necessary for the force of eight groups envisioned. Wingate moreover specified British and Gurkha troops, although he later accepted a West African brigade on an 'experimental' basis. Regular Indian infantry, however, were out – Wingate described the Indian Army in fact as 'second-rate troops.' Auchinleck's reply, on 19 August, pointed out that to be useful, LRP groups had to operate in conjunction with an advance by main forces. The administrative problems that he had earlier brought to London's attention meant there could be no such advance from Assam until March 1944, and he flatly disbelieved in the likelihood of a Chinese advance in strength from Yunnan. Furthermore, the army in India, in the midst of retraining and reorganization, would be disrupted yet again, because meeting Wingate's demands would involve breaking up one of his two British divisions, disorganizing the other by taking three battalions from it, breaking up an Indian division as well, finding over and above that 3,000 further British personnel, 600 signallers, and 'milking' units throughout India for the right sort of officer. Finally, the air support for the force would burden the already staggering Assam line of communications, while the provision of the necessary men would exhaust the reserves available both for Eastern Army and amphibious operations. Auchinleck, admitting the LRP operations could be of value, suggested that the expansion of the force be limited for the time being to bringing the 77th and 111th Brigades up to the strength

Wingate demanded, and converting one brigade of the 81st West African division, trained for jungle warfare and equipped with its own porter transport, into an LRP group. It was a formidable argument, but Auchinleck had no chance of convincing the Chiefs of Staff or the Prime Minister. The political cost of whittling down the LRP operations with which they had beguiled the Americans was too great, and the cost might well be paid in the Mediterranean. The commander-in-chief's telegram was passed to Wingate for comment, a remarkable enough procedure in itself, and drew an acid rejoinder which included the stinging phrase 'since the fall of Singapore, the war against the Japanese has been conducted from India with second-rate troops'. The Joint Planning Staff, who obviously knew which way the wind was blowing, supported Wingate, and the only concession made to Auchinleck's representations was the temporary reduction of the LRP force from eight to six groups, and Wingate's rather grudging acceptance of the 3rd West African Brigade.

On 16 September Wingate, now a major-general, returned to India to command '3rd Indian Division', the cover name for Special Force. The 70th British Division was broken up, and the equivalent of another division handed over to Wingate. Volunteers were taken from throughout the army in India, and over 600 officers and specialists arrived from Great Britain. In the same month the American 'Number 1 Air Commando', a self-contained air support unit of fighters, light bombers, transports and gliders, the fruit of American enthusiasm for the LRP concept, began to arrive in India, followed by an American LRP group, 'Merrill's Marauders', more prosaically known as the 5307th Composite Unit (Provisional). There is no question that the army authorities in India, from Auchinleck down, were less than enthusiastic about the size of Wingate's force or the special status of its commander. Churchill had told Wingate to communicate directly with him in the event of difficulties, and Wingate was not the sort of man to mitigate the effect of this open indication of the Prime Minister's distrust of the Indian military hierarchy, particularly as he shared it, and tended to ascribe difficulties to ill will or stupidity, rather than to the inherent problems of creating Special Force in complex circumstances and at short notice. The fact is that Wingate got what he had been allotted quickly enough to begin training Special Force by late October, two months after the final decision at Quebec. That by itself ought to dispose of allegations of sabotage against Wingate by orthodox soldiers, however much many of them privately disliked the man and his methods.[79]

Behind the reluctance of Auchinleck to break up British formations loomed a problem that was to bear with steadily increasing intensity on operations in South-East Asia: Britain was beginning to run out of men. As early as June 1941 the Joint Planning Staff had pointed out that existing service programmes could only be exceeded by drawing on 'imperial resources'. By November 1942 there was a recognized manpower crisis, and, when the 'manpower budget' for 1943 was settled on 11 December, the army and the RAF got little more than half the numbers they requested. Mobilization of British manpower had reached its limits by the early autumn of 1943, and the only way to meet 1944 needs was to assume the war would end that year and run down some munitions production in order to release men for the services, while the Ministry of Labour forecast an overall manpower deficit for the period January 1944-June 1945.[80] India and the Far East had a very low priority for calls on the dwindling pool of British manpower. The two British divisions there (70th and 2nd) were not likely to be reinforced, nor were their personnel likely to be repatriated soon. Wavell had already pointed out that British troops in the Far East were 'looking over their shoulder' and would regard the war as over and expect to come home when Germany was beaten. This had elicited anxious memoranda for the war cabinet from Amery and A. V. Alexander, the First Lord.[81] But no amount of paper could dispose of the facts. If British troops in India could neither be readily relieved nor replaced, it was necessary to husband them and their morale carefully, particularly for those tasks for which they were thought to be especially suitable (Auchinleck, for instance, planned to use 70th Division in an amphibious assault role). Furthermore – and this would not have bothered Auchinleck and never seems to have occurred to Churchill – if British troops were a wasting asset, more and more of the war would fall to the Indian Army (a growing proportion of whose officers were Indian), preventing any substantial reductions, and ensuring, if the 1935 Act and the promises made in conjunction with the Cripps mission had not already done so, that the old

Burma 1942-1945

Raj would never be restored no matter how spectacular the final victory.

The implications of Special Force were not the sum of Auchinleck's problems by any means. There was Stilwell, commanding the northern front – Northern Combat Area Command to the Americans – and directly subordinate to Auchinleck since he declined to subordinate himself as a corps commander to Giffard, whom he outranked by virtue of being commander of the CBI theatre. Stilwell's two original Chinese divisions had been brought up to strength by the airlift of about 30,000 men to India, and a third division was being formed. The presence of these Chinese troops, paid and fed by, but only nominally subordinate to, army headquarters in Delhi, made Amery and the Viceroy, mindful of Sino-American flirtations with the Congress Party, very uneasy. 'The greater the Chinese force, the greater the say which General Stilwell and the Americans, as patrons of the Chinese, will wish to have, not only in the conduct of the campaign but in Indian and Burmese affairs generally,' Amery wrote in a 28 June paper for the Defence Committee, adding that any attempt to curtail the Chinese presence in India would have to be made on military grounds.[82] Eden replied with a paper that stated an obvious, if not entirely palatable, truth: 'our object must be to defeat the Japanese with whatever help we can get. If we failed to do so in Burma, after having refused Chinese help, we should be open to subsequent recrimination from both Chinese and Americans.'[83] The feeling that unavoidable Sino-American participation in the reconquest of Burma would lead to Sino-American intervention in imperial relations certainly provided one of the motivations for the attempt to break away from Burma and launch out on a purely British amphibious strategy. For the time being, however, the British were stuck with Stilwell, whose Chinese divisions were probing slowly into the Hukawng valley, covering the construction of the Ledo Road, an operation which had become Stilwell's own personal war. To drive the Ledo Road on, to link it to the old Burma Road, to carry relief to China in the face of the weather, the Japanese, the British, Chiang and his own air force – this was the policy to which Stilwell was committed as inflexibly as Wingate was to long-range penetration. All the policies for Burma, however – Stilwell's, Wingate's, and Churchill's, not to mention the official

'Quadrant' decisions – hinged on a mundane but inescapable factor: administration.

There were virtually no roads worth considering in eastern India and Assam. Before 1939 no military operations had been contemplated on the north-east frontier, and the relatively sparse population and the tea gardens of Assam, the only local industry of note, had been adequately catered for by steamers on the Brahmaputra River and narrow gauge railways east of it. Between 1939-41 India's railways and inland water transport had surrendered personnel, rolling stock, and ships to improve communications in the Middle East, simultaneously with a sharp growth in the volume of movement within the country, due to India's quickening economic tempo and the expansion of its armed services. In 1942 a new front had appeared in the northeast, at the same time that shipping had to be switched from Calcutta to Bombay, putting further strain on the railroads, and a huge programme for the construction of some 200 airfields was put in hand. Over the next eighteen months the Assam line of communications had to carry material for its own maintenance and expansion, the construction of airfields, and the China airlift, and, at the same time, maintain Stilwell's Chinese corps, together with IV Corps at Imphal and XV Corps in the Arakan, to which by the 'Quadrant' decisions Wingate's corps size Special Force was added. All this had to be done in the face of shortages of equipment and adequately trained personnel, as well as the monsoon and the dislocating effect of the Bengal famine. The steady growth in the capacity of the Assam line of communications is one of the most remarkable administrative epics of the war. Nevertheless, the situation in the summer of 1943 left a great deal to be desired, particularly by the Americans, whose activities were the principal source of strain. American aid in running the line of communications was offered and, although Auchinleck was obviously reluctant, probably for the same reasons that made Amery cautious about the number of Chinese troops in India, at 'Quadrant' a directive to the new Supreme Allied Commander on administrative matters was drafted that signalized an American victory in this area as well: 'The prerequisite to the effective opening of the supply route to China is the development of the transportation system of N.E. India and Assam. This is a matter of urgency and you should in consultation with Commander-in-Chief India and the appropriate United States authorities in India plan your requirements and initiate the necessary action . . .' In the aftermath of 'Quadrant', the Indian authorities found themselves accepting American railway units for the Assam line of communications, and committed to a target of 220,000 tons per month capacity by January 1946 (by which time, if the Americans had their way, Rangoon would again be in allied hands, and the airlift and Ledo Road both unnecessary).[84]

During the five months between the end of the Arakan offensive and the assumption of responsibility by SEAC in October, the British war effort against Japan had taken its final shape, a shape that owed far more to American pressure than British wishes. At 'Trident', and more forcefully at 'Quadrant', the Americans had imposed the clearance of north Burma as the immediate objective of British endeavour. In the new structure of SEAC they had retained control of what was emerging as the single most vital commodity in the theatre – transport aircraft – and had preserved a special position for Stilwell. They were preparing to assert a greater degree of control over the communications system in eastern India. Wingate, with whom the Prime Minister hoped to satisfy the Americans, rebounded Frankenstein-like on Churchill and Brooke. Operations in north Burma alone would retain not only American confidence, but, as Marshall had made clear, American aircraft. Despite this, Churchill and the Chiefs of Staff continued to cherish the hope that an amphibious strategy would be possible, despite their palpable lack of the resources to execute such a strategy. At the same time, the Indian Army was emerging as a force capable of facing the Japanese. When the latter played into Slim's hands by launching their 1944 offensives, the way was opened not only for the counter-stroke that made possible the long-sought American goal of reopening the Burma Road, but for a culmination of Britain's war in the east that made all the strategic argumentation in London after 'Quadrant' irrelevant. This disjunction between what Churchill and his advisers (joined quickly by the SEAC planners) wanted to do, and what was actually happening, marks the remainder of the war in South-East Asia.

IV

The Attempt to Escape:
September 1943-September 1944

(i)

In an interesting repetition of post-'Trident' developments, discussion in London after 'Quadrant' focused not on north Burma, but on amphibious possibilities, particularly 'Culverin'. These discussions, however, revealed a rift between Churchill and the Chiefs of Staff that quickly became a yawning chasm. Their increasingly acrimonious and unreal argument lasted, incredibly, for the next year. In late September Churchill had told the Defence Committee that an amphibious assault on the northern tip of Sumatra was the most desirable operation for the spring of 1944.[1] Mountbatten's directive accordingly stressed operations by an 'amphibious circus', and the new Supreme Commander left London with 'Culverin' firmly implanted in his mind. These ideas quickly began to dissolve in contact with reality, however, as planning studies showed that the British simply did not have the resources for 'Culverin'. On 6 October the Joint Planning Staff finished its examination of the problem with these gloomy conclusions:

(a) The most promising operation within the resources allotted at 'Quadrant' is the capture of the Andamans. The target date could be early March 1944;

(b) The capture of Northern Sumatra in the spring of 1944 could only be carried out if considerable assistance is provided by the United States.

Even with American approval, they went on to explain, 'Culverin' could only be mounted if operations in the Mediterranean were curtailed after 1 December, the invasion of southern France ('Anvil'), scheduled to complement 'Overlord', cancelled, and inroads made on the naval support and assault shipping for 'Overlord' itself. Even if all this could somehow be done, the severe strain on the Indian base and the reduction of reserves there to dangerous levels would also have to be faced.[2] Since neither Churchill nor the Americans were willing to accept any abridgement of European operations, the logic of the Joint Planners' paper prevailed. Cancelling the operations against Akyab and Ramree that had led a ghostly existence in one form or another for eighteen months, the Chiefs of Staff nominated the Andaman Islands ('Buccaneer') as SEAC's amphibious target. Their choice had at least the merit of being on the way to Sumatra and Malaya – and far from north Burma. Churchill, however, was clearly unhappy about 'Buccaneer', shortly thereafter minuting testily 'there is only one operation [ie 'Culverin'] worth considering and we ought not to confuse the issue', but, at least temporarily, he was acquiescent.[3]

It is symptomatic of the confusion that afflicted British thinking about the war in the Far East that in an annex to their paper the Joint Planners delivered what ought to have been the *coup de grâce* to any thought of a reconquest of Burma from the north.

> The problem of maintenance along an ever lengthening and tenuous line of communication – liable to frequent interruption during the monsoon – render a campaign based on this overland advance unrealistic . . . We conclude, firstly that logistic considerations alone preclude the possibility of advancing very far into Central Burma against even a scale of opposition much below that to be expected; secondly that even if we could maintain adequate forces at the end of such long and precarious L. of C., the advantages conferred on the enemy by the nature of the terrain would certainly render an advance a slow and costly affair. In consequence, we consider that any plan based primarily on an overland advance would be unrealistic. This course is therefore rejected.[4]

Yet these same planners only two months before had thrown the weight of their collective expertise behind Wingate's proposals, which were based upon the assumption that an overland reconquest of Burma was feasible – indeed Wingate's thoughts were already racing ahead from Mandalay to Bangkok and Hanoi. Even as the Joint Planners rejected a north-south advance in Burma, Wingate's LRP forces were training in Central India to spearhead just such an advance.

In September, shortly before relinquishing operational control to SEAC, Auchinleck had drawn up a plan that attempted to carry out the Quebec directives without violating administrative common sense. The LRP groups were expected to be followed up by main forces, so Auchinleck planned an advance eastward by three divisions from Assam to the Indaw-Katha area astride the Irrawaddy in north Burma, supported by a southward drive by Stilwell's Ledo force and south-westward thrust by the Chinese armies from Yunnan (known as 'Yokeforce'). The limit of the advance was set by the furthest point at which troops could be maintained once the monsoon broke (and possibly by Auchinleck's disbelief in the offensive capacity of the Yunnan Chinese).[5] The implication of this plan was that the next dry season would see a further leap southward, for unless southern Burma was cleared and Rangoon opened, the tactical as well as the administrative situation must remain very uncertain. Burma had to be left alone or reconquered. Churchill, the Chiefs of Staff, and the Joint Planning Staff rejected both courses, and, in the end, events shaped strategy, rather than the more desirable reverse.

When Mountbatten arrived in India, he inherited Auchinleck's final plan and made it the basis of his own. Politically more astute than Wavell and very conscious of the Sino-American components of his task, the new Supreme Commander paid a visit to Chiang in mid-October and discussed his plans for the impending dry season. The Generalissimo agreed to the participation of the Yunnan armies, if the British launched an amphibious operation in the Bay of Bengal, a position he had maintained unswervingly for some eighteen months. Since the planners in Delhi were as certain as those in London that 'Culverin' was not on for 1943-44, SEAC had little trouble agreeing in early November with the Chiefs of Staff that 'Buccaneer' should be their goal. With this agreement, SEAC's 1943-44 programme took shape as follows: 'Buccaneer', an overland advance on Akyab, and a complex series of operations in north Burma. There the three-pronged converging advance by IV Corps, Stilwell, and 'Yokeforce' was to follow up Wingate's LRP formations. As a final touch the 5th Indian Parachute Brigade, which had been training for well over a year, was to disrupt the railway from Mandalay north to Myitkyina – the supply line of the Japanese division facing Stilwell.[6] This programme, if carried out, would have swept the Japanese out of north Burma, to the benefit of the airlift and the indefatigable road builders. Clear enough in itself, it still begged the question, 'What then?' No sooner did this programme seem firm, however, than new breezes blowing through the allied stratosphere began, in familiar fashion, to reduce it to shreds and tatters again.

Another allied summit was impending, and, in preparation for it, British and American planners continued the effort, on which they had been engaged since 'Trident', to hammer out an agreed strategic design for the final reduction of Japan. On 25 October, they finally produced one. The main effort would be made by the Americans in the Pacific, with the US Navy's Central Pacific drive as the *schwerpunkt* (although this was disputed by MacArthur who had claims of his own for his Army-Air Force drive in the South-West Pacific). British operations in 1944 were scheduled to be those approved at 'Quadrant'. Thereafter, however, as the expected conclusion of the European war released British resources for the Far East, the Combined Planners proposed a totally new orientation for the British war effort in the east. A British fleet would be built up in the South-West Pacific based on Australia, together with a four division striking force, for which, however, there would be initially only a one division assault lift. RAF strength would likewise be redeployed to the South-West Pacific, with the possibility that some would be used in the North Pacific as well.[7] This strategic prospectus had one great political flaw. It reduced the British Empire's contribution to the defeat of Japan to that of an auxiliary to a secondary American thrust, and, as such, would have little appeal to the Prime Minister. Politics apart, there was also the question of the administrative feasibility of constructing large base installations in Australia, whose economy was at full stretch to cope with its own war effort and the demands of MacArthur's American forces.

Both the plans taking shape in SEAC and those sketched by the Combined Planners were taken up at the three conferences held in rapid succession at Cairo, Teheran, and then Cairo again in November-December 1943. The outcome of these conferences demonstrated once again how poorly the SEAC area would do in competition with European, especially Mediterranean, needs. It also showed how large an element of fantasy there was in the wish, expressed by the Chiefs of Staff in a minute to Churchill shortly after 'Quadrant', to treat the Americans to the same sort of information about SEAC affairs as the British got about the Pacific.[8] The Americans treated the Pacific as their own affair because they could afford to – they did not need, nor really want, the British there. The British, on the other hand, could not avoid American views on SEAC because they needed American assistance there and elsewhere. This disparity in resources and bargaining power was quickly demonstrated in the argument over who should attend the first conference at Cairo, and what should be discussed there.

It came as very unwelcome news to the British that the Americans proposed to invite the Generalissimo. The British wanted a preliminary Anglo-American meeting in order to have an agreed position before the first tripartite meeting of the war. Roosevelt, on the other hand, was more concerned with establishing a relationship with Stalin, and wanted to avoid the impression that the British and Americans were settling things in advance. The President knew that Churchill and the British, in the last resort, had no choice but to cleave to him, whereas Stalin was outside his control and needed careful handling. The President also wanted Chiang at the summit, for none of the disappointments of the war had altered his belief that China would emerge one of the great powers of the future, replacing the fading European hegemony in Asia. Since Chiang could not be brought to Teheran – Stalin, not at war with Japan, declined to meet him – the Generalissimo was added to the Cairo cast. The Generalissimo's presence, to discuss the war in Asia, would also make the meeting look less like an Anglo-American attempt to concert matters before meeting Stalin – a consideration not lost on Roosevelt. Since Chiang would be present, Mountbatten had to come as well, and SEAC's plans became, willy nilly, part of the agenda.[9]

The meeting was therefore rather strained. Churchill was uninterested in China and irritated by the Generalissimo, whose presence was a defeat for him. Brooke, as his diary entries make clear, was deeply suspicious of Chiang and even more so of Madame Chiang, while he found the Chinese generals maddening and useless.[10] At the first plenary session, Chiang demanded British naval operations in the Bay of Bengal, a demand that

Churchill brushed aside. However, Mountbatten's plans, which had the approval of the Chiefs of Staff, included just such an operation, 'Buccaneer', and Roosevelt was doing little more than restating this when he promised the Generalissimo on 26 November that an amphibious assault would be mounted in the Bay of Bengal in the next few months. With the past in mind, he may have hoped also to constrain the British to turn promise into performance. All looked set fair for 'Buccaneer'.[11]

Teheran changed all that. Churchill quickly discovered, if the first Cairo conference had left him in any doubt, that Roosevelt would not act as part of an Anglo-American partnership in dealing with the Russians, and that 'Overlord' had become set in concrete, as had its complement, 'Anvil'. The Prime Minister was, however, determined to preserve enough flexibility in the Mediterranean to mount an amphibious operation in aid of the Italian advance, largely British and wholly congealed in the mountains south of Rome. The obvious source of the landing craft he needed was SEAC's 'Buccaneer'. He was aided by the promise Stalin made that Russia would enter the war with Japan once Germany was beaten. In Roosevelt's eyes this changed a number of things, including the military importance attached to Chinese (and, even more, British) assistance, in ending the Japanese war. Once back in Cairo to clean up the discussions on the Far East left over from before Teheran, Churchill set to work, using the demands of 'Overlord'-'Anvil', to convince the Americans that amphibious operations in SEAC should be dropped in favour not only of the great operations scheduled for the spring but of retaining a pool of landing craft in the Mediterranean that would allow an amphibious 'cat's claw' in Italy. His desire to restore some momentum to the Italian advance was sharpened by the knowledge that, henceforth, it would be the only British controlled theatre in Europe.[12] As far back as 'Quadrant', Churchill had realized that command of 'Overlord' would have to go to an American. Now that American had been named – Eisenhower, not, as the British had expected, Marshall. He would be replaced in the Mediterranean by General Sir Henry Wilson, with Alexander commanding the 15th Army Group in Italy. Churchill did not intend to allow their front to stagnate, not, as is sometimes alleged, merely out of chauvinism, but out of a realization that he needed every card to maintain waning British influence on the Americans. In his endeavour to sink 'Buccaneer', he was assisted by the enormous resources demanded by SEAC for it. Although subsequently very critical of the margins for which Mountbatten asked, the Prime Minister found them very useful to him in Cairo.[13] (In fact the margins were actually smaller than those employed by the Americans in the Pacific, and even Wingate, with whom Mountbatten had been bidden to consult, agreed they were reasonable, doubtless because he, like Mountbatten and Auchinleck earlier, realized that SEAC's first amphibious venture *had* to be successful.[14]) Roosevelt, to whom in the last analysis 'Overlord'-'Anvil' and the *rapport* he believed he had begun to establish with Stalin was more important than the Bay of Bengal, replayed his March role. In spite of Stilwell's advocacy, he wired Chiang on 6 December cancelling 'Buccaneer'. Chiang in reply asked for more planes – and a billion dollars in gold. 'Buccaneer's' demise of course meant replanning by SEAC. Since 'Yokeforce' was now unlikely to advance, the IV Corps advance was scaled down to a limited move forward to the Chindwin (symbolically 'Tarzan' became 'Gripfast') – something that made the LRP operations rather pointless since there would now be no main force follow up. In place of 'Buccaneer' a lesser operation, 'Pigstick', would be mounted on the Arakan coast to assist the perennial overland advance on Akyab. Even these new plans, however, did not last long. As Churchill and the British planners began to examine closely the requirements of both 'Anvil' and 'Shingle', the Anzio landing that Churchill was determined upon, it became apparent that the Mediterranean would require not most but all of Mountbatten's amphibious resources. On 30 December the Chiefs of Staff withdrew what little had been left to SEAC after the second Cairo conference. With this, 'Pigstick' collapsed as well. SEAC was left with its Arakan offensive ('Cudgel'), a minor advance in north Burma, whatever Stilwell's Chinese could do – and Wingate.[15] It was a programme that, soberly considered, made no sense, except upon the premise that SEAC had to do something. None of these operations led the British anywhere they wanted to go. Chindit II, like Chindit I, was now being launched into a void, but Wingate still represented a point of agreement with the Americans. The British could not, politically, kill both 'Buccaneer' and 'Operation Thursday', particularly as they were about to make a major effort to stake their claim to participate in the 'real' war against Japan.

The outline plan sketched by the Combined Staff Planners in October only came up for discussion at the very end of the second Cairo conference, as all the participants hastened to adjourn and with Churchill, under his doctor's increasingly anxious eye, sickening for the near-fatal bout of pneumonia that prostrated him a few days later. The assembly of a British fleet in the South-West Pacific by June 1944, together with an army and RAF contingent based on Australia, was tentatively approved, with its corollary that the major British effort for 1944 would nevertheless still be made in the SEAC area. Since SEAC had just been deprived of the capacity to mount substantial amphibious operations, that decision in turn meant 'a strenuous and wasteful campaign in North Burma for the sake of building a road to China of doubtful value.'[16] It was a situation Churchill was soon to bend his mind to changing.

Convalescent in Morocco by Christmas, the Prime Minister presided over a series of discussions that shaped the Anzio landing and incidentally stripped SEAC of its last vestiges of amphibious capacity. On 30 December the Chiefs of Staff in London sent two signals – the one to SEAC already mentioned, ordering the westward movement of its remaining assault shipping, and another to Churchill, containing the draft of a cable to Australia and New Zealand about the administrative measures necessary to support a British force in the South-West Pacific. This apparently innocuous footnote to the Cairo decisions touched off a nine-month struggle involving Churchill, the Foreign Office, the War Cabinet, and the Chiefs of Staff in what the Prime Minister later described as 'the only considerable difference I and the War Cabinet had with our trusted military colleagues.'[17] The official historian called it 'the most serious disagreement of the war' within the British high command.[18] Churchill rebelled at the idea of reducing the British role in Japan's defeat to that of mere auxiliaries of the Americans – auxiliaries that he knew perfectly well the Americans neither needed nor wanted. He felt as well that the political implications for the future of British power in Asia would be disastrous – and he never accepted that Britain no longer had a lengthy future in Asia. The Chiefs of Staff had no desire, of course, to be mere understudies to the Americans, but working on three assumptions – that the European war would end by 31 December 1944, that the pace of the American advance in the Pacific would not accelerate too rapidly, and that the necessary base area could be built in Australia – they believed that they could assemble a large enough force in the South-West Pacific to make a major British contribution in an area of Commonwealth concern whether or not the Americans liked it, and, moreover, to make it without the six-month time lag that would be involved in transferring huge forces from Europe after Germany's defeat to the SEAC area for 'Culverin' and successive operations there. From a professional point of view as well they wanted to be in on the kill when the Americans reached the Japanese home islands. From their respective positions neither the Prime Minister nor the service chiefs budged for months. Their lengthy argument was conducted with all the rancour and intensity that tired and harassed men can generate.

Churchill had no sooner returned to London than he took the initiative. When the Joint Planning Staff presented the Combined Chiefs' of Staff plan, agreed upon at Cairo, to a Defence Committee meeting of 19 January, the Prime Minister immediately declared that this was the first he had heard of the matter. Technically incorrect, his claim may be substantially true if both the state of his health and his European preoccupations at the second Cairo conference are recalled. In any case, he clearly had no intention of being bound by the Pacific section of the final report he had initialled at Cairo. He reminded the Committee how cool Admiral King had been at Quebec to the offer of a British Pacific fleet, and told them 'he was dismayed at the thought that a large British army and air force would stand inactive in India during the whole of 1944.' This undesirable state of affairs could be avoided by mounting 'Culverin', and planning for it ought therefore to continue. If, of course, a superiority of six or eight to one was demanded on all occasions amphibious operations became impracticable, he added sarcastically, in a jab at 'Buccaneer's' corpse. He also remarked, reflecting a long-held view, that since the Russians might enter the war at any time after the end of 1944, the Pacific thrusts might well become less important.[19] He found support for his view from the Foreign Office, which entered the discussion a month later with a paper on the diplomatic consequences of the strategy embodied in the Cairo decisions. As far back as 14 December, Eden had reminded the House of Commons that the British were 'still principals in the Far Eastern War', and the Foreign Office note made a number of powerful arguments in favour of the Prime Minister's position. An auxiliary role to the Americans in the Pacific was unlikely to have much attraction to the British public when they were asked to continue the war after the German surrender. Directly engaging and defeating the Japanese army in South-East Asia would have a greater effect on Asian opinion, by discrediting the Japanese military and restoring British prestige, than anything that might happen in the remote reaches of the Pacific.[20] Like Churchill, the Foreign Office looked forward to a post-war Asia in which Britain would continue to wield considerable influence. Two days before the Defence Committee meeting at which he threw down the gauntlet to the Chiefs of Staff, Churchill had sent them a memorandum on one of his favourite themes – the reduction of the Indian Army. Wavell and Auchinleck, the Prime Minister wrote, ought to 'rely as much as possible on the martial races . . . get back to the high standard and efficiency of the prewar Indian troops', increase the 'officer, and particularly the white officer cadre', all in the interests of an army based on 'really trustworthy fighting recruits.'[21] Clearly the Prime Minister had more than current operations in mind, as he showed a few months later when he spoke approvingly to the War Cabinet of Amery's plan to resume European recruitment for the Indian Civil Service and Indian Police, which had been suspended in 1939. It was necessary to maintain the strength and quality of the European element in the Indian services, he commented.[22] In his heart neither he, nor many of his colleagues, accepted the logic of the 1935 Act and the Cripps mission, not to mention the Indian war effort itself.

Further support for the Prime Minister's desire to make SEAC the centre of the imperial war effort in the east came, understandably, from the Supreme Commander and his staff. After the cancellation of 'Buccaneer' had led to a curtailment of operations in north Burma, Mountbatten's planners produced a new design, calling for a redefinition of SEAC's mission. They wanted to abandon the Ledo Road project and fall back on the airlift to sustain China, concentrating all of SEAC's effort on mounting 'Culverin', followed by a drive through the Straits of

Malacca to the South China Sea.[23] To argue the case for this repudiation of both the Quebec and Cairo decisions, Mountbatten sent a team of planners (the 'Axiom' mission) headed by his American deputy chief of staff, Major-General A. C. Wedemeyer, to London early in February, carrying with them a paper putting the new SEAC position in terms bound to find a receptive audience.

A major amphibious and airborne assault on South Burma would be unavoidable were we to persist in establishing direct and overland contact with China. The forces required would comprise far more than the present resources of SEAC. Once committed, they would be relatively ineffective in quickening the tempo of a Pacific advance, and ill-placed to develop an alternative major thrust against Japan. The whole of Burma must eventually be purged of the enemy, but an attempt at this time to recapture Burma will not hasten the end and may well delay it. This is not the propitious time to embark on major military operations designed to reconquer Burma.

Relief from all but minor commitments in North Burma necessary for the defense of the air route will free resources of SEAC for other operations calculated to accelerate the Pacific offensive.

Conclusion.

Land contact with China through North Burma will gain no timely advantage to us or to China, and will commit us in Burma to costly and sterile effort, thus retarding rather than hastening the defeat of Japan. On the other hand, the air route commits us only to the limited operations necessary for its defense, thereby freeing forces for more productive effort against Japan.[24]

That effort would be 'Culverin' and its successors. Even as Wingate wrote hopeful memoranda about an advance to Bangkok and Hanoi, and as his brigades stood poised to enter Burma, SEAC was repudiating the strategy that alone gave LRP operations any meaning. The SEAC staff hoped to launch 'Culverin' in November 1944, and make the next leap, to Singapore or the Sunda Straits, in February 1945 – if resources arrived on time from Europe. They planned to reach French Indochina by November 1945.[25] The choice of Wedemeyer to head the 'Axiom' party indicated that Mountbatten expected the stiffest opposition to his proposals from the Americans, and Wedemeyer confirmed this in a note for Churchill.

I anticipate difficulty in my homeland with regard to our recommendation to the effect that the Ledo Road project should be discontinued and that we should concentrate our efforts on ensuring continued flow of supplies to China via the air ferry route. I would appreciate your support in this regard. I feel we are on logical ground in that our strategy as now envisaged would provide early sea communications to China, which, in the final analysis, is the most effective means by which we can import sufficient tonnage to support a large scale air offensive from China and, in addition hasten the economic assistance promised by the President to the Generalissimo.[26]

Churchill's support, while a foregone conclusion, did not assure SEAC's proposals of a smooth passage in London, for they were caught in the increasingly sharp conflict between the Prime Minister and the Chiefs of Staff. Wedemeyer's party and the Joint Planning Staff, after considerable wrangling, finally agreed that only if Germany was beaten by 1 October could 'Culverin' be mounted as early as March 1945, with the recapture of Singapore and the advance into the South China Sea coming in the spring and summer of 1946. The same paper conveniently showed that the Pacific strategy espoused by the Chiefs of Staff would bring the allies to Japan's doorstep six months sooner than the SEAC proposals.[27] Churchill simply denied the validity of the calculations involved. In any case, he was not prepared to be shifted by staff studies from what he believed to be not only strategically desirable but politically necessary. When the 'Axiom' mission departed for Washington, they could, therefore, only carry word that British strategy for the Pacific was still 'under consideration'.

The Joint Chiefs of Staff were ready for Wedemeyer. Stilwell, naturally distressed at the proposal to close down his war in north Burma, had dissented strongly from the SEAC recommendations and sent a mission of his own to Washington to say so. He could do this without being technically disloyal to the Supreme Commander, since in one of his many *personae* he was not Mountbatten's subordinate. The 'Axiom' mission also had the misfortune to arrive just as a new American design for the Pacific was taking shape. Its most striking feature was a sharp acceleration of the operational timetable, one that would bring American forces to Formosa by February 1945. What the British did in the Pacific, or whether they did anything at all, mattered even less now than before. In support of their final assault on Japan, however, American planners intended to launch a devastating strategic bombing offensive by the new B-29 Superfortresses, some of which were to be based on airfields near Calcutta and in China. 'Drake' as this concept was christened, required not only a road but a pipeline into China. The reason had changed, but the road through Burma still dominated American thinking, and the 'Axiom' party could make no dent in the Joint Chiefs' position. On 21 March the American service chiefs told their British counterparts that clearing north Burma should be Mountbatten's goal for 1944 – as it had been the American goal from the beginning.[28] Wearily Wedemeyer and party prepared to return to England.

In London, meanwhile, the argument between the Prime Minister and the Chiefs of Staff dragged on. The one new factor was the transfer of the main Japanese fleet from its home waters to Singapore in late February. Undertaken to bring that fleet closer to its oil supplies and so conserve Japan's dwindling tanker tonnage, the move nevertheless gave Japan potential command of the Bay of Bengal and provided an argument against mounting amphibious operations there. The Prime Minister, however, quickly dealt with this argument by pointing out that the threat posed by preparations for 'Culverin' would pin the Japanese fleet to Singapore and aid the American advance. In a major paper circulated to the Defence Committee on 3 March, the Prime Minister summed up his position, especially its political aspects, impressively.

A decision to act as a subsidiary force under the Americans in the Pacific raises difficult political questions about the future of our Malayan possessions. If the Japanese should withdraw from them or make peace as the result of the main American thrust, the United States Government would, after the victory, feel greatly strengthened in its view that all possessions in the East Indian Archipelago should be placed under some international body upon which the United States would exercise a decisive control. They would feel with conviction: 'We won the victory and liberated these places, and we must have the dominating say in their future and derive full profit from their produce, especially oil'.[29]

This paragraph, with its obvious concern for the future of the entire European position in Asia, was by-passed rather than confronted by the Chiefs of Staff in their answer. 'Whatever strategy we follow, the major credit for the defeat of Japan is likely to go to the Americans . . . The first mortal thrust will be the Pacific thrust, upon which the Americans have already embarked. We should not be excluded from a part in this thrust . . .'[30] Churchill's point had been precisely that the dimensions of the American victory in the Pacific made it doubly important that Britain be *seen* to liberate at least her own possessions. The exchange is symptomatic of the stage the argument had reached by mid-March, with each side denying the other's premises. Ismay tried to end the dispute by suggesting to Churchill that he impose his own strategy on political grounds, but this the Prime Minister would not do, although in fact that was the basis of his desire for 'Culverin'.[31] He had, of course, not forgotten the disastrous consequences of the belief that he had overridden professional military judgment about the Dardanelles in 1915, and wanted to beat the Chiefs of Staff – or perhaps the Joint Planners, the 'masters of negation' he had always resented – on their own ground. The argument dragged on. By April a compromise, the 'Middle Strategy', had emerged, by which British forces based on western Australia would thrust northward via Timor, the Celebes and Borneo, a strategy that had little in its favour except that it split the difference between Churchill's position and that of the Chiefs of Staff. Then the industrious Joint Planners produced a fourth variant, the 'modified middle strategy', that split the difference between the Middle Strategy and the original Chiefs of Staff position.[32]

In the midst of this, the 'Axiom' party left on its return trip to India, minus one of its members, Brigadier Geoffrey Bourne, retained by the Prime Minister to assist him in beating off the Joint Planners. Wedemeyer carried back word that there would be no resources available for an amphibious operation in SEAC that year, and 'Culverin' joined the long list of mooted, planned, and cancelled amphibious operations in South-East Asia. Pownall noted mordantly in his diary on 1 April that the Americans were

determined that our role shall be confined to developing air action from China to support the Pacific operations plus a reputed drawing off of forces from the Pacific by land action in Burma. The latter is pretty fatuous really, for nothing we do by way of a land

campaign in Burma will divert anything really important from the
Pacific theatre. A few divisions perhaps (which are not in short
supply in Japan), a few hundred aircraft, but nothing that matters.

After a week's reflection he added on the 9th:

Almost it makes one think that some [Americans] want to keep the
British from doing anything against Japan that can get any lime-
light, wanting it for themselves, and determined to put us into the
place of poor relations doing chores in the basement. This is not
at all Winston's idea, who is determined that the British shall play
not merely a useful but a very visible part in the war against
Japan. The capture of Burma, only, does not fill that bill; which
accounts for the contest now going on between him and the Chiefs
of Staff.[33]

Four months had now passed since SEAC had asked for a new
directive and a redefinition of its mission. The 'Quadrant' decisions were moribund; events on the battle fronts in the Arakan
and Assam were giving an entirely new shape to the war in
Burma. But with the British High Command locked in a bitter
internecine dispute, and Stilwell and the Joint Chiefs of Staff still
keen on the link with China via north Burma, another two
months passed before Mountbatten on 3 June got his new
directive, instructing him

To develop, maintain, broaden and protect the air link to China in
order to provide maximum and timely flow of POL and stores to
China in support of Pacific operations: so far as is consistent with
the above to press advantages against the enemy by exerting maximum effort ground and air particularly during the current monsoon
season and in pressing such advantages to be prepared to exploit
the development of overland communications to China. All these
operations must be dictated by the forces at present available or
firmly allocated to SEAC.[34]

While this directive allowed Mountbatten some degree of flexi-
bility, it stressed the American aims in SEAC rather than those
of the Prime Minister or of SEAC itself, as expressed by the
'Axiom' mission. In the light of the fierce battle raging in
London, the omission of any reference to amphibious operations
is striking – aided by events, the Americans had nailed the
British firmly to Burma, as Pownall had predicted they would.
Two days after the directive was issued, Alexander's troops

entered Rome. At American insistence much of his force was
then withdrawn to prepare for 'Anvil', a reduction that deprived
the only other British theatre of its forward impetus. The day
after that 'Overlord' was launched, opening the way for an
American build-up in western Europe that rapidly eroded British
influence in the alliance. From Casablanca until the spring of
1944 the British had fought a stubborn rearguard action for their
strategic concepts. After that date it became an undisguised
retreat.

All of this might not have been happening, as far as the argument in London over Pacific strategy was concerned. By midsummer threats of resignation were in the air, and Eden's diary
entry for 6 July catches the atmosphere.

> After dinner a really ghastly Defence Committee nominally on Far
> Eastern strategy . . . our discussion . . . was meaningless when it
> was not explosive . . . Chiefs of Staff are emphatic that resources
> are not available to do ['Culverin'] until some time after German
> war is over . . . W[inston] kept muttering that resources were
> available, but produced no evidence and ended up by accusing us
> all of trying to corner the Prime Minister or take it out of him or
> some such phrase. Finish 1 : 45 a.m.[35]

Brooke noted in his diary that the Prime Minister, as the discussion went against him, 'became ruder and ruder. He finished
by falling out with Attlee and having a real good row with him
concerning the future of India. We withdrew under cover of this
smoke-screen just on 2 a.m., having accomplished nothing beyond losing our tempers and valuable sleep.'[36]

Gradually, however, reason – or at least the pressure of events
– made its weight felt. First an examination of the dual requirements of the Fleet Train needed to make the Royal Navy
self-sustaining in the Pacific (something the Americans were
insistent upon), when added to the immense requirements for
shifting base establishments from India and the Middle East to
Australia, proved to be beyond British shipping resources. (It is
characteristic of the whole argument that the Admiralty, the War
Office, and the Ministry of War Transport could not produce an
agreed figure for the tonnage required.) Then the American Joint
Chiefs of Staff, on their mid-June visit to London, showed themselves both indifferent to British operations in the South-West
Pacific and uninterested in helping the British cope with the

supply problems their Pacific strategy would entail, since the American advance across the Pacific was now accelerating so rapidly that the Americans could more profitably use their own resources to keep up its momentum.[37] Finally the Australians proved less than eager for a British theatre, with a British commander, based on their territory. Churchill cabled to John Curtin, the Australian Prime Minister, in mid-August 'I am deeply concerned at the position that would arise in our Far Eastern Empire if any considerable American opinion were to hold that America fought a war on principle in the Far East and won it relatively unaided while the other allies did very little towards recovering our lost property.'[38] The reply indicated how little the Australians still identified with Churchill's fading 'Far Eastern Empire' and where they thought their future security lay. Australia did not wish to have its existing relationship with MacArthur disturbed, Churchill was told.[39]

If both 'Culverin' and the various Pacific strategies were equally impossible, what could be done? Mountbatten, summoned home by Churchill for consultations during the last stages of his herculean struggle with his military advisers, brought SEAC's answer – exploit the disastrous Japanese defeat in Assam by pressing forward to Mandalay and mounting a combined airborne and amphibious assault on Rangoon.[40] It was not quite what Mountbatten, let alone Churchill, had originally wanted; but at least it was not the Pacific strategy, and it was *almost* within the compass of SEAC's resources. The Pacific strategy, save for the lingering notion of a Commonwealth Task Force in MacArthur's barony, followed 'Culverin' into the shadows. On the eve of the second Quebec Conference in September, the British had, finally, an agreed position. The Americans would be offered – again – a self-contained British fleet for the Pacific offensive, while, in Burma, the British proposed that Mountbatten be authorized to advance into central Burma ('Capital') and begin planning both for the capture of Rangoon ('Dracula') and the return to Malaya ('Zipper'). For 'Zipper', four Indian and two British divisions would be moved east as soon as possible after the German surrender, which, in the August euphoria generated by the allied surge across northern France, then seemed imminent. Preliminary American reaction to all this followed a predictable pattern – the offer of the fleet was ignored, a Commonwealth Task Force in the South-West Pacific viewed favourably at the moment when (or possibly because) the Australians and MacArthur were killing the idea, and Mountbatten's plans accepted, subject to the reminder that it was the clearance of north Burma that really interested the Joint Chiefs.[41]

'When history comes to be written,' Ismay had remarked in a letter to Pownall in May, 'I believe that the waffling that there has been for nearly nine months over the basic question of our strategy in the Far East will be one of the black spots in the record of British Higher Direction of War, which has, on the whole, been pretty good.'[42] Viewing the argument in thirty years' perspective, it is hard not to agree. It should have been evident after 'Quadrant' that the British were facing a tough battle to be allowed even a symbolic role in the Pacific war, and that a major contribution was out of the question. It is little short of incredible that no one looked into the administrative implications of the Pacific strategy, much less sought Australian views, until months into the argument. Of course by 1944 the war was in its fifth year. All the British participants were tired men, and had immense problems weighing upon them – the preliminaries of 'Overlord', the flying bomb threat, the prolonged Anglo-American argument over 'Anvil'. For the Prime Minister, there was the growing consciousness of diminishing British resources and influence, even as his post-war fears and concerns grew sharper. And, when all allowances have been made, his position in the controversy was more logical – if often intemperately put and clouded by attempts to beat the planners on their own ground – than that of his opponents, for the Prime Minister never lost sight of his political goal, which was to extract from the thoroughly unsatisfactory state of affairs in the east a British victory that would repair some of the damage done by earlier defeats. While it can be objected that this was beside the point, that all the European empires in the east were in a terminal state, Churchill at least preserved some relationship between his military strategy and his political goal, illusory as that goal ultimately turned out to be. It is difficult to see to what end the Pacific strategy would have led, beyond the gratification of the Chiefs' of Staff natural professional desire to be 'in at the kill'. But if 'Dracula' and 'Zipper' bore some resemblance to 'Culverin', that was the result, not of Churchill's powers of persuasion, but of the course of events in Burma where the war took a shape and momentum that dragged all of the planners after it.

(ii)

While the strategic controversy raged in London, Mountbatten had to contend with the bizarre structure of SEAC, which even Marshall admitted was administratively unsound, the jarring personalities inadequately contained within it, and the problems of dealing with the impact of a battlefield situation whose complexities and fluctuations accentuated the inadequacies of the SEAC structure. It was his greatest achievement as a supreme commander that he did all this so well that Slim could concentrate on fighting and winning the great battles of 1944-45.

The anomalies in SEAC started right at the top. Stilwell was both part of the command structure and simultaneously outside it, able to use one position at will to nullify the other, as he did over the 'Axiom' mission. SEAC's integrated Anglo-American staff, headed by Lieutenant-General Sir Henry Pownall, who was put in by Brooke to keep Mountbatten 'on the rails', contained a large planning staff, separate from those of Mountbatten's three service commanders because Churchill, Brooke, and the Americans had become wary of the inevitably negative conclusions produced by the planners in India and wanted Mountbatten to have independent advice. So Delhi, already crammed with the Government of India and the Indian Army, became in the autumn of 1943 host as well to SEAC headquarters and those of two of Mountbatten's three service commanders. The latter introduced three more complications.

The creation of SEAC led to the abolition of Eastern Army, and Giffard was promoted to command 11th Army Group. Theoretically, he should have functioned as Mountbatten's land forces commander. Stilwell, however, who found British army officers like Wavell, Alexander, and Giffard much harder to accept than men like Auchinleck and Slim from the socially less prestigious Indian Army, refused to subordinate himself, as commanding general on the northern front, to Giffard. He agreed, however, to accept orders from Slim, Giffard's principal subordinate, but only until his advance reached Kamaing in north Burma. What would happen then was left obscure. This incredible arrangement actually worked, largely because Slim, as he later admitted, never gave Stilwell an order he knew the prickly American would not accept. The virtual repudiation of his authority by the Americans was bad enough for Giffard, but he found it impossible to work with Mountbatten. Pownall described him as 'an estimable and high principled man whom everybody likes', but added, 'he *is* a tired man . . . has been long abroad and he dislikes Mountbatten so much that he won't "play".' Six months of friction culminated in Mountbatten's decision in May to ask Brooke to replace Giffard.[43] Mountbatten's relations with Admiral Sir James Somerville, after a smooth start, became equally difficult. Somerville was senior to Mountbatten in the Royal Navy and Pownall at least was certain that this lay at the root of the quarrel. 'Somerville,' he confided to his diary, resented 'a junior officer of his own Service put in to command him . . .'[44] Some of Somerville's actions may have given colour to Pownall's theory, but there was certainly far more to the dispute than a mere clash of personalities. Somerville felt that Mountbatten's headquarters and planning staffs were unnecessarily large and usurped functions that belonged to SEAC's service commanders. He also simultaneously denied that he *was* merely one of Mountbatten's commanders in chief, since the Admiralty had reserved the right to communicate with Somerville, whose area of responsibility stretched well beyond SEAC's boundaries, directly and without Mountbatten's knowledge. This, the Royal Navy's official historian later admitted, was one of the principal sources of the Somerville-Mountbatten row, since it gave the Admiral support for his claim to partial independence while depriving the Supreme Commander of the full control he felt entitled to exercise. By June 1944 matters had reached a point where Mountbatten referred his problems with Somerville to the arbitration of the Chiefs of Staff. A potentially very embarrassing situation resolved itself painlessly, however, since Admiral Sir Percy Noble, the head of the Admiralty delegation in Washington, had asked to return home and the First Sea Lord had recommended Somerville as his successor. Churchill approved, and Somerville went to a trying and vital job in the United States, where he was most successful. His replacement was Admiral Sir Bruce Fraser, and 'the difficulties experienced by the Supreme Commander in achieving a satisfactory working arrangement with the naval command in his theatre thereafter evaporated.'[45] Air Chief Marshal Sir Richard Pierse, the third of the trio, had been in the east since early 1942. Replaced as Air Officer Commanding, Bomber Command, after a series of disastrous operations at the end of 1941, he had been posted east of Suez, first as Wavell's air chief in ABDA, and then as air officer commanding in India. Described by one shrewd colleague as capable but lazy, and by Pownall as 'not intelligent', Pierse encouraged Giffard to try to assert his independence of Mountbatten, and then supported the Supreme Commander's decision to sack Giffard.[46] It is an interesting reflection on the true priority SEAC enjoyed in London that it took a year to replace Mountbatten's original ill-assorted troika of commanders with men who had not only ability but the willingness to work in harness.

Many of the other problems SEAC encountered initially were also unavoidable, given the peculiar nature of the command. The story that Mountbatten had an officer on his staff whose sole duty it was to check details of the Supreme Commander's dress and appearance before any public function is surely apocryphal, but it is clear that Mountbatten's large personal staff was in part a reflection of the Supreme Commander's realization that raising morale was his first, and perhaps paramount, task. Carefully staged tours, publicity, attention to the 'showman' aspects of his role – all the things in fact Somerville deplored – were important here, much as it all may have fitted Mountbatten's expansive personality. The SEAC staff may have been excessively large, duplicating that of the three commanders-in-chief and causing friction with GHQ, India, but the problems Mountbatten had with his commanders-in-chief certainly would not have disposed him to rely exclusively on their planners, while Pownall felt that the whole atmosphere at Delhi had become one of *non possumus*. A symbolic break with the past came when SEAC headquarters moved to Kandy in Ceylon in April 1944, leaving behind India Command's legacy of defeat and, typically, Giffard and Pierse, who kept their headquarters in Delhi. The move symbolized as well the amphibious orientation Mountbatten hoped to give SEAC's strategy, and, ironically, it took place just as 'Culverin' was passing into the shades. While the move of his headquarters was within the Supreme Commander's power, replacing discordant personalities and altering the clumsy structure of SEAC could only be done gradually, while some things could never be effectively grappled, because they represented divergent American views and interests over SEAC's role and goals. In these areas Mountbatten had to accommodate to what he could not change.

One of the most marked of SEAC's peculiarities, one not found in either the Mediterranean or SHAEF, was the existence of independent national baronies within a theoretically integrated allied command. Stilwell's unique position was only the most obvious of these. The reservation of control over American transport aircraft in SEAC to the Joint Chiefs (who exercised it through Stilwell) was another. A third area where the Americans made themselves felt was in the control of the Assam railways. Auchinleck had first refused American help in running them, then agreed under pressure and subject to the overall control of the Indian railway authorities. Mountbatten, whose Principal Administrative Officer was the American Lieutenant-General Raymond Wheeler, decided very quickly to accept the American offer to take over and run some of the more troublesome sections of the Assam line of communications. These three things together illustrate a point Pownall made in a letter to Ismay in late April, about Marshall's habit of communicating directly with the American generals in SEAC.

> There are other signs that the N. Burma business is being regarded as a 'CBI Theatre' (that expression has actually been used), and there is a tendency apparent to short circuit not only this Head-quarters but also British Chiefs of Staff under whose orders we are.
>
> I do not suggest this is done 'of malice aforethought', but the Americans are so dead set on their Aid to China line of business that they will adopt any means to their end, and will listen to no argument. If they don't get satisfaction in one quarter they seek it in another.[47]

The most important of the special provisions the Americans made to ensure their satisfaction was the retention of control over the bulk of SEAC's transport aircraft.

The British decision in 1940 not to build their own transport aircraft has already been mentioned, and in October of that year Britain concluded an agreement with the United States for the purchase of transports. Their allotment of American production in 1941 was 9 percent. In January, June and December 1942, the agreement was reaffirmed, but the British share dropped to 7 percent that year. Meanwhile, in March, Brooke had begun to put pressure on Air Chief Marshal Sir Charles Portal, the Chief of the Air Staff, to provide enough 'Bomber Transport' (ie, converted bomber) squadrons to lift three airborne divisions. Portal, struggling to maintain the bomber offensive in the face of Admiralty demands on behalf of Coastal Command, as well as the needs of overseas theatres, stoutly resisted. But by the winter of 1942-43, it was plain that the British hope of drawing all their air transport requirements from the United States was vain, and they began building their own. Throughout 1943 repeated protests and reminders only got Britain 11 percent of American production, while their own fledgling programme yielded a mere 209 aircraft. In the first six months of 1944, a further 476 came off British production lines, but most of these were earmarked to lift the British airborne component of 'Overlord'. The United States, therefore, remained the principal source of supply for SEAC.[48] When Pierse formed Headquarters, Air Command South-East Asia, in December 1943, his Troop Carrier Command was led by an American, Brigadier-General W. F. Old, despite the fact that four of Old's six squadrons were RAF. These squadrons had to meet the needs of India as well as the Burma front, and, in fact, only one could be considered constantly available for air supply in Burma. Most of the transports in the SEAC area were outside Pierse's command, however. Colonel Philip Cochrane's Number One Air Commando had twenty-five transports – thirteen of the invaluable DC-3 (C-47 or Dakota) and a dozen of the larger C-46 or Commando. The latter could carry 10,000 pounds of freight, or 35 fully equipped troops, as opposed to the Dakota's 6,000 and twenty-six, but only the Dakota was manoeuvrable enough to do supply dropping. Cochrane's force, however, as Marshall had made clear, was in South-East Asia to support Wingate. The largest body of transports by far, some 230 Dakotas and Commandos by September 1943, belonged to the fifteen squadrons of the United States Air Transport Command, flying the China airlift from fields in north-east Assam.[49] At the first Cairo conference, when large scale offensive operations in north Burma were still expected, Mountbatten was authorized to divert 1,100 tons a month (about 50 percent of Air Transport Command's capacity at the time) to support his offensive, and was assured that in an emergency he could count on drawing planes from the airlift.[50] The permission lapsed when 'Tarzan' collapsed and, although the promise remained, the machinery for implementing it was characteristically clumsy, since Mountbatten had to ask the Joint Chiefs in Washington for permission through Stilwell. If the Deputy Supreme Commander had been available in Delhi, this would have been reasonable enough, but in December Stilwell, always happiest in the field, betook himself to the northern front to direct the operations of his Chinese divisions. He was thus inaccessible at precisely the moment when the ability to use air supply became critical, as Slim faced a major Japanese offensive in the first test not only of the new Indian Army, but of the new SEAC structure as well.

When Giffard moved up to 11th Army Group, Slim replaced him temporarily at Eastern Army, and then became commander of the newly formed Fourteenth Army that replaced it. Slim's responsibilities were immense: Lieutenant-General A. F. P. Christison's XV Corps in the Arakan and Lieutenant-General G. A. P. Scoones's IV Corps in Assam, as well as Special Force when it entered Burma and vague control over the Ledo Chinese. While planners in London and Delhi dreamed of amphibious assaults that would have reduced Fourteenth Army to minor operations on the frontiers of Burma, Slim and his corps commanders prepared to push forward in the offensives finally sanctioned at the second Cairo conference. As they did so, however, signs began to accumulate that the Japanese were preparing an offensive of their own.

The original Japanese plans of 1941 had not included any operations beyond the frontiers of Burma, which would become the western bastion of the Co-Prosperity Sphere. The speed and ease of their victories had, however, produced symptoms of the 'victory disease' in Burma as elsewhere, and, in August 1942, Field-Marshal Count Terauchi's Southern Army Headquarters in Hanoi ordered Fifteenth Army in Burma to plan a limited offensive into Assam to disrupt the reorganization of the Indian Army and exploit the Congress Revolt in India. The plan (Plan 21), which was recognized as administratively risky, was abandoned in December, as the American offensive in the South-West

Pacific made steadily mounting demands on Japanese reserves.[51] Chindit I, revealing both the mounting offensive potential of the British, and the penetrability of even the tangled country on the India-Burma frontier, coincided with a reorganization of the Japanese commands in Burma that brought a very offensive-minded soldier to the fore. Burma Area Army Headquarters was set up at Rangoon and Fifteenth Army at Maymyo passed into the hands of Lieutenant-General Renya Mutaguchi, an ambitious soldier who promptly proposed to revive Plan 21. His chief of staff, who knew a great deal about administrative problems, opposed him. He was promptly sacked and replaced by an officer fresh from Tokyo, whose inadequate knowledge of administration was matched by great enthusiasm for Plan 21. In June 1943 Burma Area Army approved Mutaguchi's proposals and the following month both Southern Army and Imperial General Headquarters accepted the idea of an offensive into Assam.[52] The latter hoped for a political as well as a military dividend from the operation. From the masses of bewildered Indian prisoners taken in 1941-42, and from the large Indian population of South-East Asia, the Japanese had formed an Indian Independence League and an Indian National Army, in the hope of exploiting unrest in the subcontinent. Both these organizations were galvanized by the arrival from Berlin of Subhas Chandra Bose in May 1943. A charismatic Bengali radical, he had been Congress Party president in 1938, but had broken with Gandhi the following year. An advocate of direct action against the British under the slogan 'Give me blood and I promise you freedom', he was unable to reconcile himself to Gandhi's subtler tactics. Briefly arrested early in the war, he fled India in January 1941 and made his way to Germany, where he broadcast to India and set to work organizing an Indian Legion for the Germans from prisoners taken in North Africa. Then came an invitation from the Indian Independence League to lead the 'Free India' movement in South-East Asia. Bose left Kiel on a U-boat in February 1943, transferred to a Japanese submarine off Madagascar, and reached Tokyo in June. The Japanese Government, although it did not place great hopes on what Bose might accomplish, was happy to see him try. Returning to Singapore, Bose proclaimed himself head of a Provisional Government of Free India, and commander-in-chief of the Indian

National Army, one of whose 'divisions' (about 7,000 strong) would accompany Mutaguchi's expanded version of Plan 21, now known as the '*U-GO*' offensive.[53] While the Japanese did not expect the 'March on Delhi' actually to materialize, any wavering in the morale of the Indian Army caused by the presence of the 1st INA Division, or any unrest Bose could spark off in India, would be pure gain.

In its final form the Japanese offensive consisted of two separate but closely related operations. In the Arakan, the new Twenty-Eighth Army would mount an offensive (*HA-GO*) against XV Corps, drawing in and pinning down Slim's reserves. Then Mutaguchi, with three divisions, would destroy IV Corps in the Imphal plain, seizing the great supply depots there and depriving the British of their springboard for operations into Burma. While this was taking place, another new formation, Thirty-Third Army, with two divisions, would hold off Stilwell and the Yunnan Chinese – if the latter should decide to move. The Japanese were working to very narrow administrative margins, frighteningly so in the case of the Fifteenth Army, but Mutaguchi counted on the *élan* of his men to carry the day – after which he could subsist from captured British dumps. It was, after all, what had happened in 1941-42.[54]

It was Mutaguchi's misfortune that the army he hoped to defeat no longer existed. Slim had made it plain on taking over in October 1943 that units cut off were henceforth to stand fast and rely on air supply. The changes in army organization and training, and the new spirit Auchinleck, Savory and Slim had fostered, were aimed at ensuring that when isolated units stood and fought, it would be to good effect. As signs of a Japanese offensive mounted, Slim ordered his Principal Administrative Officer, Major-General A. H. I. Snelling, to put the air supply organization on alert to supply XV Corps by air, and the packers began to work around the clock. Despite all the warnings the British had, however, the Japanese, using only one of Twenty-Eighth Army's two divisions, opened their offensive in February with a stunning tactical surprise, slashing into the rear of the 7th Indian Division, overrunning the divisional headquarters, and then surrounding much of the XV Corps 'tail' in what became known as the 'Admin Box'. A year before, such a blow would have guaranteed a Japanese victory. Now the divisional commander, Major-General F. W. Messervy (an old hand at having his headquarters overrun – the Germans had done it twice in North Africa), made his way into the Box, whose heterogeneous garrison of infantrymen, gunners, and rear-area troops formed a new version of the old square and stood firm.

Messervy's division went onto air supply, and, in 714 sorties over the next five weeks, the tireless Dakotas showered down 2,300 tons of everything from ammunition to mail, razor blades and *SEAC,* the theatre newspaper (the latter, edited by Frank Owen, formerly of the *Evening Standard,* was one of Mountbatten's morale-building innovations). The degree of air superiority necessary for uninterrupted aerial resupply had been assured when, in November 1943, the Spitfire finally reached South-East Asia and the RAF at last had an aircraft capable of outmatching the Zero. The incredible valour, which had served the Japanese so well before, now turned against them. Without armour or air support, with only a week's supplies of his own and deprived by the stubborn defence of the Admin Box of those he hoped to capture, the Japanese commander battered on as the traditions of his service required, while Slim brought up four divisions to hammer the Japanese against the anvil provided by his two forward divisions. Slim later wrote for the official historians an account of the mood in which he fought this battle. 'This was to be our first major test against the Japanese in our come-back, and I was not prepared at that stage to undertake it on equal terms. I wanted the greatest superiority I could get. Completely to destroy a Japanese offensive would, I thought, have the greatest moral effect on our troops.' He accomplished what he set out to do. The Japanese force attacking the Admin Box alone lost 5,000 of its 8,000 men. For the first time since 8 December 1941, the Indian Army had won an unequivocal victory. It was the turning point of the war in Burma.[55]

Air supply played a critical role in the Arakan victory and this prefigured the future, as did the problems in arranging it. The resources available to Troop Carrier Command's six squadrons could not meet all the demands made on their 126 planes. In February alone, in addition to supplying 7th Division in the Arakan, they had to fly in 4,200 tons to Stilwell's Ledo force, nearly 1,100 to the 81st West African Division in the Kaladan valley on the inland flank of XV Corps, as well as meeting some of the demands of Special Force and of isolated detachments in the Chin Hills and at Fort Hertz, delivering in all 7,995 tons in 3,011 sorties.[56] This meant that every available plane was in the air virtually every day. There were nearly 700 transport aircraft in the theatre by mid-February, but most belonged either to Wingate's Air Commando or to the airlift. To ease the strain on Old's squadrons, Mountbatten by-passed Stilwell, who was not available anyway, and on 18 February asked the Chiefs of Staff to approach Washington for authority to take thirty-eight Dakotas from the Hump route. The Americans agreed, but only on 24 February, the day the Japanese gave up their assault on the Admin Box.[57] The lesson of the relatively limited Arakan operations was clear: air supply was crucial, its demands would quickly outrun British-controlled resources in a crisis, and reference to Washington, via London took far too long. The next stage of the Japanese offensive showed Mountbatten had taken the lessons to heart.

U-GO opened in the second week of March, just as the Arakan offensive was fading out. The Japanese had sprung a tactical surprise in the Arakan, and they did it again in the first stages of the Imphal battle, moving farther faster than Slim had anticipated. As a result the 17th Indian Division south of Imphal was forced to fight its way back into the plain, relying on air supply as it did so. With six divisions drawn into the Arakan operations, Slim was off balance, and the consequences might have been serious but for the Dakota. Slim decided to move the crack 5th Indian Division (a pre-war regular division with a splendid North African record behind it) from the Arakan to Imphal, but the normal rail/road transfer would take much too long, while Troop Carrier Command could not manage a fly-in in addition to its other commitments. The answer was another levy on the airlift, but here a problem presented itself. Mountbatten had already tapped the airlift once for the Arakan operations and again to support the fly-in of Wingate's Special Force. After the second occasion, he had received a message from Roosevelt that enough was enough. Now, on 14 March, Slim was appealing urgently for twenty-five to thirty transports to shift 5th Division. Conscious of the delays that had occurred on previous occasions, Mountbatten had proposed to Stilwell some time before that authority to draw on the airlift be vested in Lieutenant-General Daniel Sultan, Stilwell's deputy, who was accessible in Delhi, but no arrangement on these lines had been made as yet. On the 15th Slim repeated his request, and Mountbatten, who had given preliminary orders the preceding evening, made one of his most important contributions to the Burma campaign, taking a decision that only his personal standing with the Americans made possible and that would have been difficult, if not impossible, for Wavell or Auchinleck. He sent two telegrams to the Chiefs of Staff, the first announcing that, on his own authority, he had taken thirty Dakotas off the airlift and would keep them for a month. He pointed out in the second that during the Arakan crisis he had tried for three days to get Stilwell's approval and then waited a week for a reply after he had referred the request to Washington through London. He concluded by asking for standing authority to divert aircraft to meet operational emergencies. This opened a lengthy telegraphic battle that paralleled those raging about Imphal. As Slim won his battles, Mountbatten fought constantly to prevent operations from being crippled for lack of the new wonder weapon, the DC-3, fast becoming to Burma what the LST was in the Mediterranean. Anglo-American arguments there, based on differing strategic approaches and to some extent on differing political aims, often were fought out on the technical issue of the movement of those ungainly but invaluable amphibious workhorses, because it was less disruptive than arguing the underlying differences. In SEAC transport aircraft emerged in 1943-44 as the key to overland campaigning – the only kind of campaigning as it turned out that SEAC could expect to conduct. Since British and American aims in South-East Asia, military and political, diverged more widely than they did in Europe, the tussle was correspondingly sharp.

The Americans accepted Mountbatten's *fait accompli*, having no other choice, but refused his request for automatic 'drawing rights' on the airlift, softening this by agreeing that the Supreme Commander could deal with Sultan when Stilwell was immured on the northern front. No sooner had transport for the 5th Division been assured than the battle took a new twist, increasing the demand for air transport. As one of Mutaguchi's divisions moved toward the road connecting Imphal with the railhead at Dimapur, Slim decided to switch most of Messervy's 7th Division north as well. The movement of two divisions, air supply to the Imphal plain, and support for Stilwell and Special Force needed far more than the thirty Dakotas Mountbatten had already taken – at least seventy more in fact. That large a diminution of the airlift, bringing trouble with Chiang and Chennault, the Americans would not consider. Mountbatten's request for more transports coincided with the last stages of the 'Axiom' mission's pilgrimage, and, certain now that the British were committed in North Burma, the Americans offered a very considerable increase in SEAC's air transport resources. General Arnold proposed to send four 'combat cargo groups' of 100 aircraft each to Burma at monthly intervals beginning on 1 July. This, while useful in the 1944-45 campaign, was of little immediate help, and the Americans suggested that the seventy-plane gap could be bridged by drawing on British transports in the Mediterranean theatre. The sequel to this neat reminder that there were other sources of Dakotas besides the airlift is interesting. In Italy Alexander was preparing to launch his final offensive to break the stalemate around Cassino and take Rome – his last chance to do it before 'Overlord'. The Chiefs of Staff were very reluctant to remove anything at all from him. In the end, complicated juggling produced enough transports from the Mediterranean (most of them American, however) and the Joint Chiefs agreed Mountbatten could keep the thirty he had borrowed from the airlift as long as the battle required them, although they simultaneously pared down Arnold's original offer to two transport groups, a decision communicated to Stilwell and only reaching Mountbatten indirectly through Sultan.[58] Adequate air transport and supply capability was assured until 15 June, but it had been a close run thing. The Chiefs of Staff obviously expected the Americans to support the Burma campaign that was really their idea, while the Americans clearly feared that if the British could draw automatically on the airlift, it would be reduced to a trickle.

Mountbatten's success in conjuring up the planes meant Slim could fight the battle secure in the knowledge that air movement of essential supplies and reinforcements was assured, regardless of what happened to land communications. It was fortunate that he could, since the Japanese cut the Imphal-Dimapur road at Kohima at the end of March. By then, however, the airlift was in full swing. 5th Division was flown into Imphal, followed by a brigade of the 7th; Messervy's headquarters and a second brigade, plus a brigade of 2nd British Division were lifted to the Dimapur area to join Lieutenant-General Montagu Stopford's XXXIII Corps in its drive south to relieve Kohima and open the road to Imphal. 'Operation Stamina', the support of IV Corps in the Imphal plain from 18 April to 30 June, flew in 19,000 reinforcements and 13,000 tons of cargo, while taking out 43,000 non-combatants and 13,000 casualties. At its height, in the second half of April, fifteen squadrons with 384 Dakotas and twenty Commandos were involved – five American squadrons from the airlift and five from the Middle East, plus five RAF squadrons (one of them on loan from the Middle East as well).[59] It is interesting to note that at Stalingrad, air supply to the German Sixth Army, initially some 300,000 strong, averaged 90 tons a day in December 1942 and 120 tons a day in January. By contrast, Scoones's smaller force got 148 tons a day in April, rising to 362 in June. Air supply, made possible by borrowed resources, turned Imphal-Kohima into a Stalingrad in reverse for the Japanese Fifteenth Army. Starting with supplies for only twenty days, the Japanese needed to capture Imphal by the end of March. When they failed to do so, their administrative situation became steadily worse, while the whole ethos of the Imperial Army, reinforced by Mutaguchi's personality, forbade breaking off the offensive. Not until 8 July did Mutaguchi and Lieutenant-General Masakazu Kawabe, at Burma Area Army, finally accept defeat. By that time, inadequate supplies and medical facilities, the monsoon, and its stubborn persistence in a hopeless task had ruined Fifteenth Army. Of the 84,000 men who began *U-GO*, 53,000 became casualties (over half of them fatal). The 30,000 remaining were, for the most part, walking wounded, malaria-ridden or suffering from malnutrition – but only some 600 allowed themselves to be taken prisoner. The Indian National Army's debut had been a fiasco and, by the end of the Imphal battles, the Japanese were using what was left of it as porters. Slim's casualties were 16,700, of whom only a quarter were fatal, while SEAC's total casualties from January to June amounted to 40,000 plus 282,000 who went sick, although most of the latter recovered and returned to their units.[60] Slim summed it all up when he later wrote that the 'Fourteenth Army had met picked Japanese troops in straight bitter fighting and had beaten them. Our troops had proved themselves superior in battle to the Japanese . . . This was the real and decisive result . . . They had smashed forever the legend of the invincibility of the Japanese Army. Neither our men nor the Japanese soldier himself believed in it any longer.'[61]

Simultaneously with the decisive series of battles in the Arakan and on the central front, Wingate mounted 'Operation Thursday'. No episode in the whole war in Burma has given rise to so much controversy as Chindit II, and the argument (like that over T. E. Lawrence) shows no indication of dying down. Certain facts, however, seem clear. Wingate had had his greatest impact on the war in 1943. Chindit I had boosted morale, demonstrated conclusively the potentialities of sustained air supply while improving the techniques for using it, and started the Japanese command in Burma along the road that led them to Imphal and ruin. At Quebec Wingate made his greatest impact on the politics of the war, enabling Churchill and Brooke to convince the Americans that they took north Burma seriously at a time when they felt it critical to reduce the causes of Anglo-American friction in the interest of agreement on the Mediterranean. Having played Wingate, and by their success secured further American resources for SEAC, Churchill and the Chiefs of Staff were stuck with him, although both intended the degree of commitment in north Burma to be minimal since both had strongly-held, if divergent, views on the proper British strategy against Japan and the overland reconquest of Burma figured in neither prospectus. After 'Quadrant', however, Wingate's operations began to slip more and more out of focus. Originally conceived as opening the way for the advance of 'main forces', Special Force became steadily more anomalous as it became clear, first that the main forces were not likely to advance, and then that a Japanese offensive was impending. By this time Wingate's ideas were also changing, and he now thought in terms of air supported 'strongholds' that, like medieval castles, would become centres and rallying points for his columns, protected by 'floater' columns waiting outside to take any would-be attacker in the rear. But the attempt to hold territory was not what the LRP brigades had been designed for, and was bound to deprive them of the assets of dispersion and mobility that had been their strength, and ultimately their salvation, during Chindit I. Wingate's memoranda of 10 and 11 February 1944, proposing an air-supported LRP advance to Bangkok and Hanoi, can be seen as an attempt, in the face of increasingly adverse circumstances, to keep his strategy central in SEAC.[62] If, however, Wingate's operations became increasingly beside the point by early 1944, they were virtually impossible to abort. Politically it would be taken badly by the Americans, something neither Churchill nor Mountbatten wished. Furthermore, having created Special Force (which absorbed a sixth of SEAC's best infantry), Mountbatten and Slim naturally had hopes of deriving some value from it. Chindit II, therefore, went ahead, making heavy demands on SEAC's air transport resources, but too late to have any effect on the mounting of *U-GO*, while Wingate's death in an air crash on 24 March deprived the operation of the leadership, drive and vision that, at his best, he was unquestionably able to supply. Thereafter, the Chindit operations, although an epic of courage and endurance, became irrelevant to the decisive battles taking place about Imphal and Kohima. They never contained even half their own numbers of Japanese troops, while their casualties, employed as they were far longer than Wingate had ever intended, and in a role unsuitable to their organization and equipment, soared. The final blow came when they were moved north to assist Stilwell's drive. Ruthlessly used by Stilwell – as was the American LRP unit – they were on the verge of collapse when finally evacuated to India in July.[63] Although Special Force was not formally disbanded until February 1945, the July evacuation marked the end of Chindit operations. Wingate's significance lies in his political and psychological impact. Militarily, it is hard to disagree with the official historians who concluded that 'Special Force was a military misfit; as a guerilla force, it was unnecessarily large and, as an air transported force, it was too lightly armed and equipped either to capture strongly defended vital points or to hold them against attacks by forces of all arms until the arrival of the main forces . . . in spite of the fortitude and gallantry of the LRP troops, the results achieved were not commensurate with the resources diverted to it at the expense of the 14th Army.'[64]

Between February and July, that Army had won a decisive battle. But what use would or should be made of the victory?

In London the Prime Minister and the Chiefs of Staff were still locked in their futile battle over Pacific strategy. The Americans remained wedded to clearing north Burma, in the interest now of 'Drake'. Mountbatten, newly installed in Ceylon, had faced the disappointment of his amphibious hopes, but out of events on the central front was fashioning a new two-stage programme for 1944-45. 'Champion' would be a converging advance on Mandalay by Slim and Stilwell, who had reached Kamaing in June and whose front was now directly subordinate to Mountbatten since Stilwell still declined to take orders from Giffard (now, in any case, a lame duck). 'Champion' would require more air transport than Mountbatten had, and would mean maintaining forces in central Burma once the 1945 monsoon broke. Avoidance of this administrative problem was the rationale for 'Vanguard', a combined airborne and amphibious operation to take Rangoon. 'Vanguard', in its turn, however, would require still more transport aircraft, as well as naval assault forces and two more divisions.[65] 'Champion-Vanguard' promised only the reconquest of Burma, always far more an American than a British objective, and did not comply with Mountbatten's 3 June directive in which both his British and American masters bade him to make do with the resources he had. Like all SEAC's amphibious projects, 'Vanguard' was founded on the hope that the necessary resources would come from Europe in time, although they never had before. There was another conceivable alternative to 'Champion-Vanguard' which was not even considered: to do nothing more in Burma, giving the air resources back to the Hump airlift and letting Stilwell try to finish his road, while conserving the Indian Army and the few British formations in SEAC for the major amphibious operations in pursuit of British goals that the end of the German war alone would make possible. This would have been consistent with not only Churchill's thinking and that of the Chiefs of Staff, but with Mountbatten's original ideas. The obvious objection to this course of action was that the Americans would not have liked it and would have put intense pressure on the British to keep moving in Burma. By midsummer 1944, however, the American advance in the Pacific was moving at *blitzkreig* speed. In June they had landed in the Marianas and destroyed the Japanese carrier air arm in the battle of the Philippine Sea. The Marianas campaign ended the following month, as did MacArthur's 'leap frog' advance in New Guinea. The Americans now had a platform for their B-29s, and were poised on the threshold of the Philippines. Japan was facing total defeat, a fact signalized by the fall of General Hideki Tojo's government. What happened in SEAC was no longer very important, especially as the significance of China as the base for 'Drake' had also waned. The Joint Chiefs of Staff and the President would certainly have objected to abandoning the effort to restore contact with China – it was, after all, a presidential election year – but there was another, all British, reason as well for pressing on in Burma, and one operating with greatest force at the SEAC level. The British Empire had finally tasted victory in a theatre where nothing but defeat and frustration had hitherto been its lot, and the victorious Fourteenth Army had acquired a momentum which its driving commander had no intention of allowing to slacken. The war in Burma was turning into a peculiar sort of sideshow – an almost private war between Slim's army and the Japanese, in which the political object of the campaign was less important than simply winning it. Mountbatten was affected as well, since it began to look as if victory in Burma might be the only victory in SEAC's grasp.

Slim, now Sir William for his Imphal victory, had believed from the beginning that it would be necessary to fight through the monsoon, to keep up pressure on the Japanese (and perhaps to keep the campaign alive). From July through November, through drenching rains and liquid mud, past the debris of the beaten and exhausted Japanese Fifteenth Army, Lieutenant-General Sir Montagu Stopford's XXXIII Corps pushed on toward the Chindwin and across it to gain the springboards for the next dry season campaign. 'Some of what we owed we had paid back', Slim wrote later. 'Now we were going on to pay back the rest – with interest.'[66] But the first payment was exacted not from the Japanese but by the monsoon from XXXIII Corps. Of its average weekly July–November strength of 88,500, about half were maintained forward of Imphal in pursuit of the Japanese. Total casualties, however, came to 50,300, of whom only forty-nine were killed in action. More than half the 47,000 who went sick had to be evacuated back to India. Even with mepacrine, there were over 20,000 cases of malaria.[67] By August, however, when Mountbatten took 'Champion-Vanguard', re-christened 'Capital-Dracula', to London, the stage was set for the final, if now strategically irrelevant, stage of the war in Burma. The campaign Churchill had never wanted to fight was about to conclude in a way he had always deprecated.

V

Burma Reconquered
September 1944-May 1945

(i)

The last eight months of the war in Burma were not paralleled by the intense Anglo-American arguments that had marked its earlier stages. For one thing, the major decisions had all been made, by the allies or by events. The relative ease with which decisions affecting SEAC and the Pacific were reached at the only major conference of 1944, the second Quebec conference ('Octagon'), contrasts sharply with the arguments that marked the conferences of the previous year. Moreover, as the war drew to a close Churchill had worries enough at home and in Europe, without concerning himself deeply with the affairs of a theatre that had become, strategically and politically, a dead end.

The British came to Quebec with a programme for the Far East based upon the proposals Mountbatten had brought with him to London in August – 'Capital', 'Dracula', advanced planning for the British return to Malaya, plus a British fleet for the Pacific and a Commonwealth Task Force to operate from Australia. On the eve of the first plenary session, Churchill sent a minute to the Chiefs of Staff, in which he harmonized, to his own satisfaction, what the British would propose at 'Octagon' with what he had advocated during the nine-month struggle with his military advisers in London.

> . . . our policy should be to give naval assistance on the largest scale to the main American operations, but to keep our own thrust for Rangoon as a preliminary operation, or one of the preliminary operations, to a major attack upon Singapore. Here is the supreme British objective in the whole of the Indian and Far Eastern theatres. *It is the only prize that will restore British prestige in this region.*[1]

He commented later that he wanted the Empire's lost Far Eastern possessions won back on the battlefield by British arms and not handed back by the United States after an exclusively American victory – not least perhaps because of his concern over whether or on what terms they would then be returned.[2] The competing forces acting on him and on British strategy were emphasized again, however, by Churchill's desire not to allow 'Dracula' to interfere with the Italian campaign, where Alexander's advance was again slowing down as it encountered the last German mountain defences in front of the Po Valley. For the Prime Minister victory in the British-controlled Mediterranean theatre, above all victory for the Eighth Army, had become immensely important – the last chance, after Eisenhower's assumption on 1 September of direct command over all the Anglo-American forces in France, of a distinctively *British* victory in Europe. All this was reflected in the presentation Churchill made at the first plenary meeting of 'Octagon' on 13 September. He took a line that might almost be described as magnificent effrontery.

> I said that for the sake of good relations, on which so much depended in the future, it was of vital importance that the British should be given their fair share in the main operations against Japan. The United States had given us the most handsome assistance in the fight against Germany. It was only to be expected that the British Empire in return should wish to give the United States all the help in their power toward defeating Japan.[3]

Then he repeated formally the offer of a British Pacific fleet, which he had discussed with Admiral William Leahy, Roosevelt's personal Chief of Staff, the preceding day. The President interrupted his remarks 'to say that the British fleet was no sooner offered than accepted,' but Churchill, perhaps for the benefit of Admiral King, asked twice more whether the British offer was accepted, extracting first an ambiguous answer – perhaps the President had also remembered King – and then a clear affirmative from Roosevelt. He also mentioned the British desire to put a force of 600-800 Lancaster bombers into the final onslaught on Japan, and the possibility of a Commonweath Task Force in the South-West Pacific. The President replied to this by making soothing noises about 'Culverin'. All this was discussed further the following morning by the Combined Chiefs of Staff. King, in a quite incredible display of obstinate petulance, tried to reverse

Roosevelt's decision, first refusing to agree that the President had actually accepted Churchill's offer of a fleet, and then niggling about where it would be employed – 'no specific reference to the central Pacific had been made.' Only when it became apparent that Leahy would not support him, and had instructions from Roosevelt to that effect – 'Admiral Leahy said that if Admiral King saw any objections to this proposal he should take the matter up himself with the President' – did King subside. Portal, Arnold and Marshall quickly agreed that an RAF force in the Pacific was a matter for future study, while an Australian-based Commonwealth Task Force, unwanted by MacArthur or the Australians (although King suddenly saw merit in it, as a way of keeping the British away from his war), faded away.[4] A new directive for Mountbatten, replacing the anodyne 3 June document, was agreed to very quickly (SEAC's proposals having been conveyed to the Joint Chiefs of Staff before the conference and a draft directive drawn up).

1. Your primary objective is the recapture of all Burma at the earliest date. Operations to achieve this object must not, however, prejudice the security of the existing air supply route to China, including the air staging post at Myitkyina, adequate protection of which is essential throughout.
2. The following are approved operations:
   (a) the stages of Operation 'Capital' necessary to the security of the air route *and the attainment of overland communications with China.*
   (b) Operation 'Dracula'.[5]

The italicized phrase was added on the 14th at American insistence, drawing from the Prime Minister at the final plenary session the comment that, while he accepted the obligation to open communications with China, 'any tendency to overdo it would rule out our assault on Rangoon,' which was now his operation of choice for SEAC in 1945.[6]

It was not, however, the Ledo Road but events in Europe that sent 'Dracula' the way of all SEAC amphibious operations. Since November 1943, the assumption for planning purposes had been that Germany would be beaten by the end of 1944. 'Dracula' depended on the accuracy of this projection, for to mount it three divisions and two brigades would have to be withdrawn from Eisenhower's command, as well as three Indian divisions from the Mediterranean, between September and November 1944. Naval forces, assault shipping and 190 transport aircraft would also have to be drawn from Europe, leaving a mere 360 transports and 550 gliders to be borrowed from the Americans, which raises the question of who was overdoing what.[7] Even as the President and Prime Minister conferred at Quebec, however, the foundations on which 'Dracula' had been built were eroding. Churchill had been sceptical as far back as January about the possibility of finishing the German war in 1944 and, amidst the excitement that gripped everyone as the allied armies streamed across northern France and swept into Belgium, he remained a dissenter from the view that Germany was on the verge of collapse. His scepticism was rapidly justified. Eisenhower's advance, having temporarily outrun its supplies, came to a halt on the borders of Germany, while the German armies rallied. Operation 'Market-Garden', Montgomery's attempt to capture the Rhine bridge at Arnhem and so keep up the momentum, was launched on 17 September and had failed by the 25th. At the same time, Alexander's advance stalled before the Gothic Line. The European war would last one more winter. On 2 October Churchill and the Chiefs of Staff agreed that 'Dracula' would now have to wait until after the 1945 monsoon, and with this decision, the last possibility that Fourteenth Army's campaign would be by-passed evaporated.[8]

The continuation of the war in Europe further aggravated the already severe British manpower crisis. The RAF had already been forced to release 17,000 men to the Royal Navy to allow it to prepare for operations against Japan. The only way to keep the British Army going through the attrition battles now in prospect – Eighth Army alone lost 14,000 men in the first three weeks of September – was to draw further on the RAF, those elements of the navy not needed in the Far East, and further run down munitions production as well.[9] Even so, one British division had to be broken up in August and a second in November plus three marine battalions and twenty-seven artillery regiments to keep up the infantry strength of Montgomery's other divisions.[10] In South-East Asia, the situation was worse. British infantry battalions there were, on the average, 18 percent under strength, and the already inadequate replacement pool was shrinking since the War Office could not maintain it by drafts from Europe. In

June Fourteenth Army lacked some 3,500 British infantry and the deficit was predicted to rise to 11,000 by November. In July Auchinleck, who had already reduced the number of British troops both on the North-West Frontier and held for internal security duties, and instituted a general comb-out of establishments in India as well, proposed to break up three British anti-aircraft regiments and partially disband seven more anti-aircraft/anti-tank regiments by removing their anti-aircraft elements. All this, however, would barely cover existing deficiencies. The SEAC manpower crisis was largely responsible for Mountbatten's decision to break up Special Force, whose demand for high quality infantry was great, and whose wastage rates on operations had, in some cases, reached the astronomical figure of 90 percent. In September Mountbatten's manpower problems worsened sharply when the War Office reduced the period in the east that qualified British troops for repatriation from five years to three years, eight months. This decision, although a valuable morale booster, immediately added 5,700 more men to SEAC's deficiency list. Despite the redesignation of the 36th Indian Division (which had been largely British for some time) as a British division, SEAC's British component, 30,000 men below strength by late Ocober (10,000 in Fourteenth Army) was clearly a wasting asset. The final British victory Churchill sought in SEAC would be won by the Indian Army.[11]

Mountbatten presented his new plans for making progress toward that victory to Churchill in Cairo on 20 October, whither the Supreme Commander had been summoned to meet the Prime Minister as he passed through on his way back from his third wartime meeting with Stalin. In an endeavour to salvage some movement towards Singapore from the debris of discarded plans, the SEAC staff had come up with a highly ingenious combination of operations. 'Capital' would continue, but, at the same time, XV Corps in the Arakan would resume its perpetual advance toward Akyab, capturing it by an amphibious assault in January 1945. Then XV Corps would mount 'Clinch', an amphibious assault on the Kra Isthmus to sever Japanese communications between Malaya and Burma and prepare the way for the next amphibious swoop, to the Port Dickinson-Port Swettenham area in Malaya, the last stop before Singapore. In some ways it repeated the Japanese pattern of 1941-42. While all this was going on,

'Dracula' would be mounted in December 1945. How, without the use of Rangoon, the Fourteenth Army would be maintained in Central Burma during the 1945 monsoon at the end of supply lines that bent in a great loop back to Calcutta was not specified. Moreover, the plan contained the now customary element of wishful thinking. Mountbatten did not even have the amphibious troop lift for the XV Corps assault on Akyab, let alone the leap to the Kra Isthmus. The best that can be said of it is that the SEAC staff had learned of the cancellation of 'Dracula' on 10 October and had to put something together hurriedly for Mountbatten to present to Churchill ten days later. When they examined the proposals, the Chiefs of Staff prudently approved only 'Capital' and the overland advance toward Akyab, which had been going on in one form or another for over two years. They asked, however, for a new study of the Andaman Islands project, for which neither SEAC nor the Chiefs of Staff had the resources.[12]

Events in Burma again dispelled the mist of plans emanating from Kandy to mingle with the fog drifting from London. With the end of the monsoon, Slim's advance had begun to pick up speed and, by December, he was closing in on the Irrawaddy north and south of Mandalay. The Fourteenth Army staff had already worked out plans for crossing the Irrawaddy, crushing the Japanese army in the plains of central Burma, and driving south to Rangoon and the sea, the whole operation to be known as 'Extended Capital'. The September directive was already out of date and, at the Combined Chiefs of Staff meeting at Malta in late January, the British Chiefs of Staff proposed a new directive for Mountbatten, ordering him simply to clear Burma at the earliest possible date and prepare to liberate Malaya. This was the first war-time directive about South-East Asia that said nothing about China. The Americans raised no objection to this – the road to China had been reopened on 23 January when the first convoy from India reached the old Burma Road via the Ledo Road – but, their objective attained, they had little interest in seeing American resources used to attain what had now become purely British goals. For SEAC this was a serious matter since the resource in question was transport aircraft. Of the 2,500 planes in the theatre, half (1,230) were American, and the United States share of the transport fleet was much higher. The plan for 'Extended Capital' depended upon air supply. There had been serious problems already in November-December, when Slim's advance had been slowed by the diversion of American-controlled transports to China. The administrative margins to which Fourteenth Army would be working during 'Extended Capital' would be narrow enough and any disruption might have very serious operational consequences. The only way to avoid this, in the British view, was finally to give Mountbatten full control of his own transport aircraft. The Americans, who had specifically reserved control over their aircraft to themselves at 'Quadrant', and reaffirmed that decision again in January 1944, simply would not agree. Marshall made it clear why: 'United States resources required for China would not be available for operations in Malaysia.' At the first plenary session of the 'Octagon' conference Roosevelt had suggested that the British by-pass Singapore and strike at Bangkok, and Marshall's remarks at Malta made it brutally clear that the Americans had no interest in helping the British back to Singapore. They too understood its political significance. Marshall insisted that the new directive to Mountbatten be accompanied by a memorandum whose first two crucial paragraphs constituted a flat rejection of British desires.

> The primary military object of the United States in the China and India-Burma theatres is the continuance of aid to China on a scale that will permit the fullest utilization of the area and resources of China for operations against the Japanese. United States resources are deployed in India-Burma to provide direct or indirect support for China. These forces and resources participate not only in operating the base and line of communications for United States and Chinese forces in China but also constitute a reserve immediately available to China without permanently increasing the requirements for transport of supplies to China.
>
> The United States' Chiefs of Staff contemplate no change in their agreement to SAC SEA's use of resources of the United States India-Burma theatre in Burma when this use does not prevent the fulfillment of their primary object of rendering support to China including protection of the line of communication. If, in the opinion of the British Chiefs of Staff, any transfer of forces contemplated by the United States' Chiefs of Staff will jeopardize British forces, engaged in approved operations in Burma, the transfer will be subject to discussion in the Combined Chiefs of Staff.

Experienced by now in dealing with the British, Marshall added verbally that the paper 'was meant to make it quite clear that the employment of United States Forces outside Burma must be subject to fresh agreement, and that Admiral Mountbatten must not be led to assume that they would be available to him.'[13] Even through the careful language of the official minutes comes the cutting edge. The British were having their client status rubbed well and truly in. Some of the edge may have been put there by the concurrent British attempt to push Eisenhower 'upstairs', by inserting a British ground forces commander between him and control of his armies, but, whatever the reason, the British no longer had the leverage to shift the Americans, and with an insignificant alteration for honour's sake, they accepted Marshall's paper. It was the last important Anglo-American dispute about Burma of the war. Mountbatten's new directive was sent to him on 3 February. The affairs of SEAC were not on the Yalta agenda. Churchill's comment on the discussions there about the Japanese war – '. . . we were not consulted but only asked to approve' – accurately catches the minor and auxiliary status to which the British had now been reduced in that war. As if to underwrite this, Mountbatten signalled on 23 February that Slim's advance was going so well that he was cancelling 'Dracula' completely and counting on taking Rangoon from the north before the 1945 monsoon. He appended another schedule of amphibious operations, which would bring him to Singapore by March 1946 – if he got the necessary resources. In fact the war in the east was entering its last stage for the British, and they were still in Burma.

(ii)

The autumn of 1944 saw extensive reorganization at SEAC headquarters. The key to it all was Stilwell's departure in October. His relations with Chiang, never close, had finally become impossible, and he had never been able to work smoothly with Chennault, who had, of course, worsted him in the intra-American duel the previous year over China's place in the strategy of the Pacific war. He had latterly spent more and more time on the northern front where his determination to capture Myitkyina in the summer of 1944 had become obsessive, leading him to drive almost beyond endurance both Special Force and

Merrill's 'Marauders'. He had virtually ceased to function as Deputy Supreme Commander and seemed less concerned with SEAC than with warding off any threats to the completion of the Ledo Road, as he demonstrated when he utilized his direct link with Washington to argue against the 'Axiom' proposals. In any case, his work was done. He was totally identified with restoring land communications with China and that was now certain. He left as unlamented by many Americans in SEAC as he was by Chiang and the British. Not without talents, especially in the field, but an impossible allied commander, he will remain the best symbol of the fundamental disharmony of Anglo-American aims in South-East Asia. Marshall, who had appointed and supported him, immediately gave him an army command for the projected invasion of Japan.

Stilwell's multiplicity of appointments were divided among three successors, another sign of the realization of American aims. Wheeler became Deputy Supreme Commander and the Joint Chiefs' reserved powers over American transport aircraft were vested in him. Sultan replaced Stilwell on the northern front, while Wedemeyer moved from Kandy to Chungking as Chiang's new Chief of Staff. The B-29 bombers of the 20th Bomber Command, although based partly in SEAC, and the reason for the American insistence on pushing the road (and its accompanying pipeline) through to China, still remained completely outside the SEAC command structure, answerable directly to the Joint Chiefs.

Mountbatten's British team also changed completely during the autumn. Pownall's health broke down and he was replaced by Lieutenant-General Sir Frederick Browning, who had commanded the 1st British Airborne Corps in 'Market-Garden'. It was an odd appointment, since, unlike Pownall, Browning was not primarily a staff officer, but it did continue the pattern that began with Wavell in 1941 of sending east distinguished senior officers who, for whatever reason, were no longer required in the west. Giffard was replaced by Lieutenant-General Sir Oliver Leese, Bt, Churchill's candidate for overall land command in Burma eighteen months before. He brought with him from Eighth Army, which he had taken over from Montgomery, some rather Montgomeryesque attitudes. 'His staff', Slim wrote later in careful but pointed criticism, 'which he had brought with him and which replaced most of our old friends at General Giffard's headquarters, had a good deal of desert sand in its shoes and was rather inclined to thrust Eighth Army down our throats. No doubt we provoked them, for not only were my people a bit sore at losing General Giffard, but, while we had the greatest admiration for the Eighth Army, we also thought the Fourteenth Army was now quite something.'[14] Here was the origin of a tension between Leese and Slim that came to a head in May 1945. But with Leese's arrival and Stilwell's departure a more rational command structure was at last possible. Eleventh Army Group was wound up and Leese became commander, Allied Land Forces, South-East Asia (ALFSEA) with Slim and Sultan directly responsible to him. When Pierse went in November 1944, Air Chief Marshal Sir Trafford Leigh-Mallory, whose Allied Expeditionary Air Force headquarters had controlled the air support for 'Overlord', was ordered out to replace him, but died in an air crash on the way. Eventually the appointment was filled by the very capable Air Chief Marshal Sir Keith Park, ironically an early victim of Leigh-Mallory's climb to high command. Somerville departed for Washington and Mountbatten had no further trouble with the navy. With a team of commanders in whom he felt more confidence, Mountbatten dispensed with a separate planning staff, increasingly irrelevant in any case since Fourteenth Army's campaign was now SEAC's only major endeavour.

Despite Stilwell's disappearance, Mountbatten's charm, and the fact that Wheeler and Sultan were personally quite popular with the British (Pownall bestowing on the latter the ultimate accolade, 'a good honest chap'), Anglo-American relations in SEAC remained very uneasy. Pownall had noticed at a very early date that 'the Americans over the last eighteen months have rather behaved as an Army of Occupation – or if that is too strong – much as we comport ourselves in Egypt *vis-à-vis* the Egyptian Army and Government . . . there is no doubt of an atmosphere of suspicion on their part; some of their actions show it and there are many whispers which come to our ears.'[15] Time did nothing to change this, rather the reverse. Air Chief Marshal Sir Philip Joubert, SEAC's senior public relations officer, told Brooke in November 1944 that 'Anglo-American relations continued to be bad, the Americans [were] full of criticisms of our management of India and expressing openly the opinion that if they had their way there would be no British Empire after the war.'[16] Stilwell was obviously a symptom rather than a cause of the fundamental Anglo-American differences that gave SEAC's history so many strange twists. Events in China were about to provide another illustration of this.

When Chennault's plan for basing American heavy bombers in China (which Pownall sarcastically called 'tickling up Japan with B-29s') was first discussed, Stilwell had put his finger unerringly on the weak point in the air force position. Once the bombers became an irritant to the Japanese, they would mount an offensive to overrun the air bases, an offensive that the Chinese armies could not stop. Only a reorganized, and Americanized, Chinese army could protect Chennault's bases – and Stilwell put the necessary figure as high as fifty divisions. While this line of argument obviously served his purpose of asserting priority for the Ledo Road, it was a better analysis of likely Japanese reactions than the comfortable assumption that the large Japanese forces in China (one armoured and twenty-five infantry divisions in midsummer 1944) would be held off by either Chiang's army or Chennault's bombers if they decided on an offensive. And an offensive *(ICHI-GO)*, aimed at Chennault's airfields, was precisely what the Japanese decided on in January 1944. Launched in the spring, it made good progress over the summer, and, after a pause, resumed again in October. Wedemeyer, arriving from SEAC, quickly decided that the Chinese divisions in Burma were needed to stop the Japanese, and only air transport could shift them rapidly. The sequel was dramatic. 'At dawn on the 10th December I was awakened in my headquarters at Imphal by the roar of engines as a large number of aircraft took off in succession and passed low overhead,' Slim recalled.

> I knew loaded aircraft were due to leave for 33 Corps later in the morning, but I was surprised at this early start. I sent somebody to discover what it was all about. To my consternation, I learnt that, without warning, three squadrons of American Dakotas [seventy-five aircraft], allotted to Fourteenth Army maintenance, had been suddenly ordered to China . . . Passing overhead were the first flights bound for China. The supplies in the aircraft, already loaded for Fourteenth Army, were dumped on the Imphal strip

and the machines took off. *The noise of their engines was the first intimation that anyone in Fourteenth Army had of the administrative crisis now bursting upon us.*[17]

Removing the Chinese divisions from the northern front would virtually end the pressure on the Japanese there, releasing troops to confront Slim's main thrust, while the removal of the aircraft threatened the entire precariously balanced administrative structure of Fourteenth Army, at a critical moment when Slim had that army poised for his masterpiece, 'Extended Capital'.

After the Imphal-Kohima battles Kawabe and Mutaguchi were replaced. Lieutenant-General Heitara Kimura, who arrived from Tokyo to take over Burma Area Army, was the most intelligent opponent the British faced in Burma, and he needed to be. His force of roughly eleven divisions, badly mauled in the 1944 battles, faced an opponent whose skill and self-confidence were at their peak and who was emerging into the 'dry belt' of central Burma, on whose plains British superiority in the air and in armour would have maximum impact. Kimura wisely decided not to fight west of the Irrawaddy but to pull back behind the river, facing Slim with the problem of an opposed river crossing. When he realized that Kimura was not going to fight with the Irrawaddy at his back, Slim quickly recast his plan. While Sultan's remaining forces and XXXIII Corps of Fourteenth Army converged on the Mandalay area, Slim's other corps, IV, now commanded by Messervy, would move south and east to cross the Irrawaddy well below Mandalay. Once across, it would strike out for Meiktila, eighty miles to the east, the communications centre through which passed the supply lines of all the Japanese forces to the north and west. It was the boldest British plan of the war, for Slim's force was smaller than the Japanese force he proposed to disrupt and destroy in the Mandalay-Meiktila area. For its success two things were necessary: surprise, which depended on both the success of Slim's deception plan, Operation 'Cloak', and the ability of the RAF to prevent Japanese reconnaissance discovering Messervy's force during its 300-mile approach march; and adequate administrative support, which in turn meant air supply to supplement what could be hauled forward on inadequate roads or brought down the Chindwin. Once the Japanese were defeated in central Burma, air supply would become even more precious because Slim realized clearly that Fourteenth Army's rearward communications would disintegrate when the monsoon burst in May. Therefore, Rangoon had to be taken. In the second – SOB, 'Sea or Bust' – stage of 'Extended Capital', Slim proposed simply to drop his supply lines behind him and rely on air supply until he reached Rangoon. The Arakan offensive would at this point finally become a coherent part of a strategic design because, as Slim pushed south, airfields in the Akyab area would provide a quicker turn-round for transport aircraft than the receding bases in the Imphal plain. In preparation for 'SOB', Slim also began to reorganize some of his divisions. After shedding its excess vehicles two years before, 17th Indian Division was re-mechanized, to lead Messervy's push from the Irrawaddy to Meiktila, and on to Rangoon, as was the 5th (which, of course, had served in North Africa for three years and had ample experience in mobile warfare).[18]

The abrupt withdrawal of the three American supply squadrons thus came at a very awkward moment. It is curious that neither Mountbatten nor Leese had warned Slim, since Lieutenant-General Sir Adrian Carton de Wiart, who represented Churchill in Chungking, had told Mountbatten as early as 21 November that the worsening situation in China would lead to demands for the use of aircraft from Burma to shift the Chinese troops there home. Continuous consultations had gone on since then between Mountbatten, the Chiefs of Staff, and Washington, and by 5 December the SEAC air staff had earmarked two squadrons to shift two of Sultan's Chinese divisions back to China. That Slim may not have been totally surprised may be deduced from his own account. But the loss of some 1,300 sorties over the next three weeks slowed the build-up of supplies and hence the tempo of Slim's operations – by perhaps two or three weeks, he later estimated. For a plan that involved reaching the sea before the monsoon in May, winning a decisive battle of uncertain duration on the way, the loss of time was a very serious matter.[19] Pownall, in his last days as SEAC Chief of Staff, exploded in his diary, 'I'm very sorry for Mountbatten . . . He is carrying out a directive which he doesn't like, which he opposed for as long as he could, which was forced on him by the determination of the Americans . . . he is in a fair way to succeed – and then the whole thing is put into the soup by the folly of other people including particularly the Americans themselves.' A few days later he added 'unfortunately we have no clear cut political policy to match against the very plain, and aggressive US policy of aid to China (China right or wrong, useful or useless, worthy or unworthy of help).'[20]

By the time his transport aircraft were so unceremoniously removed, Slim was ready to spring a surprise of his own and, if he was not officially warned about the impending loss of his squadrons, neither were Mountbatten and Leese about the new directions in their army commander's thinking. On 18 December, Slim told his Corps Commanders, Messervy and Stopford, what he intended to do, and the next day issued his plan as a Fourteenth Army Operation Instruction. Leese had received a summary of Slim's intentions on the 17th but not until the 20th was ALFSEA sent a copy of Slim's full plan. When asked about this later by the official historians, Slim disarmingly told them that he considered the change of plan 'to be something I should do myself without asking for approval from ALFSEA or SEAC. So I did not ask for sanction.'[21] The war in Burma had become an intensely personal one – Slim and his army were going back, despite everything, and Mountbatten was simply going to have to find the necessary aircraft. Slim's confidence was not misplaced. On New Year's day Mountbatten signalled London that 'the speed of the advance into central Burma is such that 14th Army are about to enter the Mandalay Plain. Exploitation south from Meiktila-Mandalay is already under examination', he added, only slightly stretching the truth. 'The advance of the army into Burma depends absolutely on air supply,' he concluded, asking the Chiefs of Staff to persuade Wedemeyer to send the three squadrons back to him by 1 March.[22] When no immediate answer came from Washington, Mountbatten sent Browning home to put pressure on the Chiefs of Staff, who, in a curious display of detachment, tried to dissuade the Supreme Commander from doing so. Browning reached England on 15 January and, three days after his arrival, a signal went to Washington, reminding the Joint Chiefs of Mountbatten's earlier request and pointing out that failure to meet it 'may therefore well make the difference between rapid and complete victory and a stalemate . . .' After discussing the matter with Browning, Brooke noted in his diary that 'the transport aircraft belong to the Americans and . . . the reconquest of Lower Burma does not interest them at all. All they want is North Burma and the air-route and pipe-line and Ledo Road into China. They have now practically got all these, and the rest of Burma is of small interest to them . . .'[23] The Joint Chiefs, despite the prod from London, proved Brooke's point. They gave no orders to Wedemeyer but merely passed on Mountbatten's request. At last, on the 21st, Wedemeyer agreed to return two of the squadrons in a week. The third he kept. The British then moved a squadron from the Mediterranean, diverted a second which was on its way to the Pacific Fleet, and added five planes each to the establishment of the eight British transport squadrons in SEAC.[24] Slim's air supply was assured, but the whole episode showed that not only did the Americans no longer care very much about what happened in Burma, as Pownall and Brooke noted, but that London was oddly indifferent as well, something Pownall saw clearly, referring to 'lack of policy and interest amongst our own people'. After allowing SEAC to cope with the loss of seventy-five aircraft for nearly two months, and trying to avoid a personal visit from Browning, the Chiefs of Staff suddenly found eighty-five, confirming a long-standing American suspicion that the British were doing less than they could for their own theatre and counting upon American resources to make up any shortfall, something that doubtless contributed to Marshall's attitude when the Combined Chiefs of Staff met at Malta.

As signals about aircraft flew back and forth above his head, Slim pushed his forces on. His administrative situation would have shattered the nerves of a less tough and self-confident commander. He was plunging deep into central Burma, without the aircraft necessary to sustain himself there, banking upon Mountbatten's ability to find them somehow, or perhaps on the realization that none of his tiers of superiors could afford to allow his army to mire down there. By the end of January, Stopford's XXXIII Corps had closed up to the Irrawaddy and had a division across the river north of Mandalay. The Japanese, believing both British corps to be involved, were unaware of the IV Corps approach to the south. When XXXIII Corps made a second crossing, just south of Mandalay on 12 February, the Japanese were convinced that the shape of the British attack had been revealed, and began to reinforce the Mandalay area. Then, on the night of 13/14 February, Messervy put his 7th Division across at Myitche, miles to the south. The INA division guarding the eastern shore collapsed, the only significant contribution of that force to the Burma campaign. By the 21st, Messervy was ready to launch Cowan's 17th Division on its drive for Meiktila, while Stopford's forces broke out of their northern bridgehead. Six days later Cowan was on the outskirts of Meiktila, and the Japanese command had become as unhinged as had the French in 1940. The Japanese soldier still fought and died where he stood, but to increasingly little avail. On 23 February Mountbatten decided to cancel 'Dracula' and put all his cards on Slim's 'SOB' plan.[25]

The shadow of China again fell across Fourteenth Army's campaign at this point. At the meeting on the 23rd Sultan warned Mountbatten that Wedemeyer now planned to pull out most of the lone American regiment, known as 'Mars Force' and the remaining Chinese divisions in the north to spearhead a summer counter-attack in China. Not only would this relieve pressure on the Japanese by closing down the northern front completely, but raised once again the spectre of the diversion of transport aircraft. The official request to move Sultan's Mars Force to China, in aircraft already in use in Burma, came six days later. Mountbatten met Chiang on 8 March, but, in response to his appeals, the Generalissimo merely suggested he stop his advance at Mandalay. By the 27th, with the decisive battle swirling about Meiktila, Mountbatten asked Washington for a 'firm and early assurance' that he would not be deprived of any of his aircraft, which were already operating 60 percent above their normal effort. The Joint Chiefs promptly replied that the move of Sultan's American regiment would not prejudice Slim's campaign. At this point Churchill intervened, cabling on the 30th directly to Marshall, whom he correctly recognized as now the manager of the American war effort: 'As General Marshall will remember . . . we greatly disliked the prospect of a large scale campaign in the jungles of Burma and I have always had other ideas myself. But the United States Chiefs of Staff attached the greatest importance to this campaign against the Japanese and especially to the opening of the Burma Road. We therefore threw ourselves into the campaign with the utmost vigour . . . I feel therefore entitled to appeal to General Marshall's sense of what is fair and right between us . . . to let Mountbatten have the

comparatively small additional support which his air force re-
quires to enable the decisive battle now raging in Burma to be
won.' By moving the issue into the area of personal relations,
Churchill won. On 3 April the Americans agreed that Mountbatten could keep his transports until the fall of Rangoon or 1
June 'whichever date is earlier,' although he lost 'Mars Force' and
with it the momentum on the northern front. Things had changed
a great deal since the days when the Americans had used extra
air resources as bait to encourage British operations in Burma.[26]

Meanwhile, Slim's battle reached its climax. Stopford took
Mandalay on 9 March, while, after a month of confused fighting
about Meiktila, the Japanese broke off their effort to retake it
and began to retire on 28 March. Slim could now launch his
pursuit. But it was already very late. The monsoon was only
some six weeks away. The cumulative effect of the diversion of
transport aircraft to China and the slowdown on the northern
front, which allowed the concentration of Japanese forces on the
decisive struggle in central Burma, had reduced Slim's never
generous margins – temporal and administrative – almost to the
vanishing point. He still intended to take Rangoon from the
north, but regrouping before launching 'SOB' would eat up yet
more precious time. He therefore prudently provided against
failure to reach the sea in time. On 19 March he suggested a
modified 'Dracula' and, a week later, Mountbatten agreed (even
though the plan called for the use of an airborne battalion for
which he did not at the moment have the lift).[27] 'On 20 March
the Akyab airfields opened, and on 11 April Slim was ready. The
chief staff officer of the 19th Indian Division later recalled that
moment:

> . . . I stood back, wishing I had a camera, as Slim, 4 Corps Com-
> mander (Frank Messervy) and three divisional commanders watched
> the leading division crash past the start point. The dust thickened
> under the trees lining the road until the column was motoring into
> a thunderous yellow tunnel, first the tanks, infantry all over them,
> then trucks filled with men, then more tanks going fast, nose to
> tail, guns, more trucks, more guns – British, Sikhs, Gurkhas,
> Madrassis, Pathans . . . this was the old Indian Army, going down
> to the attack, for the last time in history, exactly two hundred
> years after the Honourable East India Company had enlisted its
> first ten sepoys on the Coromandel Coast.[28]

They had 300 hundred miles to go, and thirty days in which to do it. Airfield engineers moved with the armoured spearheads, to prepare the airstrips every fifty miles or so on which Fourteenth Army now depended. On the eve of D-Day for 'Dracula', Cowan's 17th Division was in Pegu, fifty miles from Rangoon. Messervy had covered 250 miles in nineteen days, in spite of Japanese resistance and the clammy pre-monsoon weather – a rate of advance that challenges comparison with the German *blitzkrieg* of 1940 or the Anglo-American dash across France in 1944. But now the rains came and Cowan's advance slowed to a crawl – it would have been far too neat, in this theatre of frustrations, for 17th Division, five of whose battalions had been with it during the 1942 retreat, to have taken Rangoon. But if 'Extended Capital' ended in anticlimax, so did 'Dracula'. On 1 May, Gurkha paratroopers dropped from American aircraft on the Elephant Point defences of the main channel leading to Rangoon. They were empty. The next day 26 Indian Division's landings began. The Japanese, however, had already left Rangoon.

VI

Barren Victory

The British Pacific Fleet, for which Churchill had struggled so long, went into operation in December 1944 and played a distinguished, if inevitably minor, role in the closing stages of the Pacific war. The RAF contribution to that war never materialized. By May 1945 the Americans had been persuaded to accept 'Tiger Force', ten squadrons to be based on Okinawa. The Americans, however, had all the bombers they needed, but by no means all the airfields. 'Problems' arose, and 'Tiger Force' evaporated. The American plans for the invasion of the Japanese home islands were never officially conveyed to the British, and an attempt by the Chiefs of Staff to discuss them with the Joint Chiefs ran into a stone wall, as the Americans showed a declining interest in the Combined Chiefs of Staff machinery after the defeat of Germany. After much pressure, the Americans did accept a three-division Commonwealth force – one division each from Britain, Australia, and Canada – to be trained on American lines and used as part of the floating reserve for the scheduled spring 1946 invasion of Honshu. Then the Joint Chiefs had second thoughts and by early August were trying to back away even from this. The decision to use the atomic bomb was exclusively American (although the development of the weapon, particularly in its early stages, had not been). The British gave the Americans a 'blank cheque'. 'The balance of power, both in the atomic project and in the Pacific, lay too heavily with the United States for the British to be able, or to wish, to participate in this decision,' wrote the official historian, while the arrangements prescribed by MacArthur for handling the Japanese surrender were intended to underline the American character of the victory.[1]

Major operations against the Japanese in SEAC ended in May 1945, although heavy fighting marked the 'mopping up' in Burma. ALFSEA continued to plan for an invasion of Malaya, under very depressing auspices.[2] The War Office, not unmindful of the impending General Election, in June lowered the time necessary to qualify for repatriation to three years, four months, without any consultation with SEAC, a decision that stripped from Mountbatten many key British personnel. Most of the remainder were aching to go home, with a corresponding impact on morale.[3] Then the Chiefs of Staff told Mountbatten that the needs of the British Pacific Fleet, and the projected invasion of Japan, in which they still desperately hoped to be allowed to participate, would have priority over anything SEAC was planning.[4] While Mountbatten's resources shrank, his responsibilities grew. In April, to free MacArthur to concentrate upon the invasion of Japan, the Joint Chiefs of Staff proposed a revision of SEAC's boundaries to take in Indochina and the Netherlands East Indies, and the change was made after the Potsdam Conference. SEAC thus inherited upon the Japanese surrender two extremely ambiguous situations and nearly a year of fighting – the old Indian Army's last twilight venture overseas. Two years after the Japanese surrender that Army, and the Empire it served, passed into history. Mountbatten presided over that transformation, together with Auchinleck. Slim, who survived a clumsy attempt by Leese to push him aside in May 1945, replaced Leese at ALFSEA and, as such, disregarded MacArthur's instructions for handling the Japanese surrender, particularly his order not to insist on Japanese officers surrendering their swords – 'General Kimura's is now on my mantelpiece, where I had always intended that one day it should be,' he wrote unrepentantly in 1956.[5] He went home to become commandant of the Imperial Defence College, and then to succeed Montgomery as CIGS in 1948, despite an intrigue by Montgomery almost as clumsy as Leese's in 1945. To the end Slim won.

But who besides Slim accomplished what they set out to do in Burma? The answer, briefly, is no one. The British, from the Prime Minister to Mountbatten, had never wanted to stage a campaign there. They were constrained to do so nonetheless both by their inability to provide the resources for the amphibious strategy they preferred, and American insistence upon reopening the road to China. If the British had been in a position to mount 'Culverin', or could have persuaded the Americans of its desirability they could – and would – have shut down operations in Burma. Lacking the capacity for the one and the persuasiveness for the other, the British could only carry on in Burma, especially since the events of 1943-44 revealed the key to their tactical dilemmas there to be the Dakota, and only the Americans could provide these in quantity. Even Churchill's use of Wingate to solve the problem of rigid American insistence on something the British believed unwise boomeranged, since it made the commitment to north Burma even firmer. The alternative of simply refusing to go into Burma was not a real one, since the British would have paid the price elsewhere, most probably in the Mediterranean.[6] In the end, in spite of everything, Auchinleck, Savory and Slim forged an army that won a victory immense but almost meaningless, except that it vindicated the Indian Army's honour and traditions before that army marched into the shadows. It certainly yielded no tangible fruit.*

The Americans also were disappointed in their aims. They hoped at first to build a great, Americanized Chinese Army; then they hoped to find a platform from which to pulverize Japan from the air. The first was impossible without simultaneously destroying the Generalissimo and was done only on a small scale by Stilwell in India. The second was overtaken by events. Roosevelt was right about the emergence of China as a great power, but it was not the China of American dreams, and its emergence after the war convulsed American politics. The Burma Road, a symbol of American aspirations, only carried some 38,000 tons between its reopening in January 1945 and October 1945, when the end of the war and the opening of Chinese ports made it superfluous – the airlift in its last month of full operations carried 39,000.[7] When the Americans reopened the road they completely lost interest in the campaign on which they had insisted and almost destroyed it in its last stages by removals, actual or threatened, of their aircraft.

On his deathbed Slim told Mountbatten, 'we did it together'.[8] They certainly wrote a brilliant page in military history, but accomplished nothing more, because the campaign had never had a realistic political goal, something that was, of course, not their fault. The European order in Asia was past resuscitation, although Churchill, who had written in 1937 '. . . my ideal is

---

* Mountbatten's considerable success in the appallingly difficult task of winding up the Raj may, of course, have owed something to the additional lustre SEAC's great victory had given to his name in Indian eyes.

narrow and limited. I want to see the British Empire preserved for a few more generations in its strength and splendour,' never accepted that.[9] An American order was equally unattainable, although over twenty-five years of bloody and expensive effort lay ahead before Roosevelt's successors finally realized it. Slim's great victory – and this is the most that can be claimed for it – helped the British, unlike the French, Dutch or, later, the Americans, to leave Asia with some dignity. That, perhaps, is no small thing.

REFERENCES

Chapter I

1 Winston S. Churchill, *The Second World War, IV*, London, 1948-54, pp.702-703

2 On the evolution of British strategy in the Far East 1919-39, see Raymond Callahan, *The Worst Disaster: The Fall of Singapore 1942*, Newark, Delaware, 1977, chapter 2, and the works cited there

3 S. W. Roskill, *Naval Policy Between the Wars, II, The Period of Reluctant Rearmament 1930-1939*, London, 1976, p.297

4 On the British response to the Sino-Japanese War, see Nicholas Clifford, *Retreat from China*, Seattle, Washington, 1967; and Bradford Lee, *Britain and the Sino-Japanese War 1937-1939*, Stanford, California, 1973

5 Roskill, *op. cit.*, p.367

6 B. Bond (ed.), *Chief of Staff: The Diaries of Lieutenant-General Sir Henry Pownall*, I, London, 1972-74, p.190

7 *Idem*

8 Lawrence Pratt, *East of Malta, West of Suez: Britain's Mediterranean Crisis 1936-1939*, New York, 1975, discusses the role of the Mediterranean in British strategy in the late thirties, and Sidney Aster, *1939: The Making of the Second World War*, New York, 1973, the commitment to containing a German thrust into South-Eastern Europe

9 Sri Nansan Prasad, *Expansion of the Armed Forces and Defence Organisation 1939-45* (Combined Inter Services Historical Section India and Pakistan, Calcutta, 1956), pp.8-9, 12, 20. This is a volume in *The Official History of the Indian Armed Forces in the Second World War*, edited by Bisheshwar Prasad. See also Compton Mackenzie, *Eastern Epic*, I, London, 1951, pp.1-9

10 Callahan, *op. cit.*, chapters 3, 4

11 On the expansion of the Indian Army, see S. W. Kirby, *et al.*, *The War Against Japan* I, London, HMSO, 1957-1969, pp.513-515; PRO, CAB 69, DO(41)19 'Note on Indian Military Problems'

165

by General Sir Archibald Wavell, 11 September 1941; CAB 66, WP (42)54 'India's War Effort' by L. S. Amery, 30 January 1942; Mackenzie, *op. cit., passim.* Philip Mason, *A Matter of Honour: An Account of the Indian Army, Its Officers and Men,* London, 1974, pp.449-70, is very good on the recruitment of the pre-war Indian Army, and the problems of 'Indianization'. The classic account of that army in the thirties is in John Masters, *Bugles and A Tiger,* New York, 1956

12 Wavell, CAB 69, DO (41)19; Kirby, *op. cit.,* II, p.48; Tim Carew, *The Longest Retreat: The Burma Campaign 1942,* London, paper ed., 1972, p.31

13 E. L. Woodward, *British Foreign Policy in the Second World War,* II, London, HMSO 1970-1976, pp.114-18; Charles Romanus and Riley Sunderland, *China-Burma-India Theater* I, *Stilwell's Mission to China,* Washington, DC, 1953, pp.3-48. This is a volume in the official series *The United States Army in World War II.* See also Barbara Tuchman, *Stilwell and the American Experience in China,* New York, 1970, pp.216-23

14 Churchill, *op. cit.,* III, p.747

Chapter II

1 Kirby, *op. cit.,* II, pp.15-16, 26-7, 30, 74

2 Lieutenant-Colonel E. I. C. Jacob, 'Operation "Arcadia", Washington Conference December, 1941,' p.27. I am indebted to Lieutenant-General Sir Ian Jacob for the use of material from his wartime diaries

3 On the 'Arcadia' conference, see J. R. M. Butler and J. M. A. Gwyer, *Grand Strategy,* III, Part 1, London, HMSO, 1964, pp.366-381; Jacob, *op. cit.,* gives a first-hand, contemporary view

4 See, for example, Wavell's signal to Hutton reproduced in Kirby, *op. cit.,* II, p.46

5 Archival information

6 Kirby, *op. cit.,* II, pp. 85-6

7 Kirby, *op. cit.,* II, pp.152-53, 176-77; Nigel Nicolson, *Alex: The Life of Field Marshal Earl Alexander of Tunis,* London, 1973, pp. 137-38, 146-47; Ronald Lewin *Slim: The Standardbearer,* London, 1976, pp.79-109. I am indebted to Mr Lewin for allowing me to read his official biography of Lord Slim while it was still in typescript, and for his kindness in discussing the war in Burma with me

8   Kirby, *op. cit.*, II, pp.17-19; Romanus and Sunderland, *op. cit.*, pp.52-7; John Connell, *Wavell: Supreme Commander 1941-1943*, London, 1969, pp.61-4

9   Churchill, *op. cit.*, III, p.607

10   *Ibid*, IV, p.119

11   Churchill to Ismay, 21 January 1942, Public Record Office (PRO), PREM 3, 168/1

12   Churchill, *op. cit.*, IV, p.120

13   *Ibid.*, p.135

14   Michael Howard, *Grand Strategy*, IV, London, HMSO, 1970, p.83

15   Connell *Wavell*, p.236

16   Butler and Gwyer, *Grand Strategy*, III, Part 2, p.484

17   *Ibid.*, p.488

18   Howard, *Grand Strategy*, IV, p.84

19   S. N. Prasad, K. O. Bhargava, P. N. Khera, *The Reconquest of Burma*, I, (Combined Inter Services Historical Section, India and Pakistan, Calcutta 1958-59), pp.17-19

20   Howard, *Grand Strategy*, IV, 84-85; Connell, *op. cit.*, pp.237-238

21   Howard, *Grand Strategy*, IV, pp. 85-86

22   *Ibid*, pp.95-96; Romanus and Sunderland, *op. cit.*, I, p.182

23   Romanus and Sunderland, *op. cit.*, I, pp.172, 182

24   Howard, *Grand Strategy*, IV, p.87

25   Connell, *Wavell*, pp.239-41

26   Howard, *Grand Strategy*, IV, pp.99-103; Romanus and Sunderland, *op. cit.*, I, pp.225-29

27   Stilwell diary 8 January 1943, quoted in H. Feis, *The China Tangle*, Princeton, New Jersey, 1953, p.53

28   Howard, *Grand Strategy*, IV, pp.106-107

29   Gwyer and Butler, *Grand Strategy*, III, Part 2, pp.625-26. Churchill, *op. cit.*, pp.374-90 contains no hint that the reconquest of Burma was even discussed, nor does the published version of Brooke's diary: A. Bryant (ed.), *The Alanbrooke War Diaries*, I *The Turn of the Tide*, London, 1957

30   See, for example, Grimsdale to Ismay, 15 August 1942, Ismay Papers IV/GRI/3; Liddell Hart Centre for Military Archives, King's College, London (hereafter cited as MAC)

31   Howard, *Grand Strategy*, IV, pp.89-91

32   Romanus and Sunderland, *op. cit.*, I, pp.250-54, 261

References

33 Howard, *Grand Strategy*, IV p.204

34 *Ibid.*, p.101

35 *Ibid.*, p.97

36 *Ibid.*, p.102

37 *Ibid.*, pp.103-104

38 COS (42) 466 (o) Final, 31 December 1942, reproduced in *ibid.*, pp.602-13

39 *Ibid.*, p.243

40 This came up at the first Combined Chiefs of Staff meeting of the conference on the morning of 14 January, and, in the words of the official historian 'the determination to satisfy the Americans on this point, indeed, was of major importance in the explicit British agreement to prosecute the war until the unconditional surrender of the Axis powers.' *Ibid.*, p.247

41 PRO, PREM 3, 146/6 contains the Roosevelt-Churchill cable of 8 January containing Chiang's complaint. The process of drafting the Prime Minister's answer of 10 January can be followed in this file and is an instructive example of the care taken by Churchill in his correspondence with the President

42 Brigadier E. I. C. Jacob, 'Operation "Symbol". Casablanca,' p.35; Howard *Grand Strategy*, IV, p.241

43 PRO, CAB 65, WM (43) 61, 29 April 1943

44 Howard, *Grand Strategy*, IV, pp.247-50. The original paper, CCS 155/1 of 19 January, and the final version, CCS 170/2 of 23 January, are reproduced in full by Howard, pp.621-22, 625-31

45 PRO, PREM 3, 143/2, Joint Planning Staff paper of 20 January 1943

46 PRO, PREM 3, 146/6, Churchill to Chiang, 25 January 1943. Earlier in the month, in another symbolic gesture, the British had joined with the Americans in renouncing extraterritorial rights in China

47 Romanus and Sunderland, *op. cit.*, I, pp.277-92

48 Anthony Eden, *The Eden Memoirs*, II, *The Reckoning*, London, 1965, p.379

49 Howard *Grand Strategy*, IV, p.403

50 *Ibid.*, pp.395-97

51 *Ibid.*, pp.10-12, 291-98, 632-36; Kirby, *op. cit.*, II, pp.301-302

52 PRO, PREM 3, 143/3/4, Churchill to Ismay, 11 February 1943

53 Connell, *Wavell*, pp.266-69, reproduces Wavell's signal of 10 February 1943 to the Chiefs of Staff, appraising them of the results

of the Delhi and Calcutta conferences. See also Howard, *Grand Strategy*, IV, pp.398-99. The minutes of the meetings are in PRO PREM 3, 143/3/4

54 Kirby, *op. cit.*, II, p.363

55 *Idem*. '. . . the Chinese . . . are naturally anxious to see the reconquest of Burma. This very fact can be made to help our plans; we can continue preparations and discussions with the Chinese on an offensive into Burma, and this will quite likely come to the knowledge of the Japanese. We shall in fact make a limited offensive into Upper Burma, with the object of confirming the Japanese of our intention to attack in Burma . . .'

56 Churchill, *op. cit.*, IV, p.831, Churchill to Ismay, 3 March 1943

57 Howard, *Grand Strategy* IV, pp.400-401

58 See the series of minutes in PRO PREM 3, 143/10, especially Churchill to Hollis, 9 April 1943

59 Kirby, *op. cit.*, II, pp.249-58, and Connell, *Wavell*, pp.241-44 discuss the background of the first Arakan offensive

60 Kirby, *op. cit.*, II, p.260, indirectly admits this, but air operations during the first Arakan offensive are nowhere discussed in detail and Kirby's summation (p.356) '. . . during this period the RAF succeeded in gaining temporary local air superiority over Arakan and in inflicting considerable losses on the Japanese,' is not very convincing in the absence of comparative figures for losses. D. Richards and H. St. G. Saunders, *The Royal Air Force 1939-1945*, III, London, HMSO,, 1953-54, p.302, admits that RAF 'operations in support of the army . . . proved singularly ineffective', but give no figures for British losses

61 PRO, CAB 66, WP (42) 54, 'India's War Effort', 30 January 1942

62 *Idem*; PRO, CAB 66, WP (43) 89, 'India's War Effort', 1 March 1943, also by Amery. These two memoranda are very valuable sources of information on the expansion of the Indian Army and its attendant problems

63 The order of the day can be found in T. Mains, *Retreat from Burma*, paper ed., London, 1974, pp.137-9; the Slim-Irwin conversation is from Lewin, *op. cit.*, p.105

64 See Lewin's remarks in *Slim*, pp.116-20; conversation with Mr Lewin, 8 June 1976

65 Connell, *Wavell*, p.239; Imperial War Museum, Irwin Papers 2/3, Irwin to Kirby, 4 January 1956

References

66 Irwin Papers 2/1, Wavell to Irwin, 9 April 1943

67 Irwin Papers 2/1, Irwin to Wavell, 9 April 1943; *Ibid.*, 'Report on visit to Maungdaw Front 4-9 May 1943', by an unidentified XV Corps liaison officer; *Ibid.*, 2/2, undated paper setting out the 'Terms of Reference' for an inquiry into the operations of the 14th Division in the Arakan. See also *Ibid.*, 2/3, 'reconstruction' of a meeting in London at Combined Operations Headquarters on 28 September between Irwin and Vice-Admiral Lord Louis Mountbatten and his chief of staff, Lieutenant-General Sir Henry Pownall. There is another summary of this conversation in *Ibid.*, 2/2

68 Irwin Papers 2/2, undated 'Most Secret' paper, written sometime after Irwin had been relieved of command of Eastern Army

69 Irwin Papers 2/1, Slim to Irwin, 18 April 1943

70 On Wingate prior to 1942 see Christopher Sykes, *Orde Wingate: A Biography*, New York, 1959, the 'official' life. On the origin of the LRP force, *ibid.*, pp.360-6; Kirby, *op. cit.*, II, pp.243-44

71 On Chindit I, see Sykes, *op. cit.*, pp.366-432; Prasad, *et al.*, *op. cit.*, I, pp.98-137; Kirby, *op. cit.*, II, pp.309-29, 499-504. There is a brilliant contemporary account by one of Wingate's column commanders, Bernard Fergusson, *Beyond the Chindwin*, London, 1945. It is interesting to compare Fergusson's later reflections on Chindit I and Wingate, given in his *The Trumpet in the Hall*, London, 1970, pp.142-61, 172-89

72 PRO, PREM 3, 143/8, Churchill to Ismay, 24 July 1943

Chapter III

1 'Most Secret' note by Irwin, undated but about 12 April 1943, Irwin Papers 2/1, Imperial War Museum

2 COS (43) 84, 22 April 1943, Public Record Office (PRO), PREM 3, 143/7

3 JP (43) 164 (Final), JP (43) 165 (Final), *Ibid.*

4 Amery to Churchill, 30 April 1943, PRO, PREM 3, 443/7

5 WM (43) 63, 29 April 1943, PRO, CAB 65

6 According to Ismay's later recollections, the suggestion that Wavell be made Viceroy was first put to the Prime Minister in the latter's White House bedroom: Note by Ismay for Churchill, 15 June 1949, Ismay Papers, II/3/158/2, MAC. The prevailing London view of Wavell's fatigue is reflected in Ismay to Churchill, 13 December 1948, *Ibid.*, II/3/128/2, MAC

7 Churchill to Ismay, 9 May 1943, PRO PREM 3, 143/7

References

8   Churchill minute of 8 May 1943, *Idem*
9   Howard, *Grand Strategy*, IV, pp.437-41
10 *Ibid.*, pp.441-43
11 CCS 242/6, 25 May 1943, printed in *Ibid.*, pp.660-7
12 *Ibid.*, p.447
13 Churchill, *op. cit.*, IV, p.701
14 Howard, *Grand Strategy*, IV, p.543
15 Churchill to Secretary of State for War, 24 March 1943, PRO, PREM 3, 143/10
16 Brooke to Churchill, 23 May 1943, *Ibid.*
17 Memorandum by Attlee for the Defence Committee, 26 May 1943, DO (43) 11, PRO, CAB 69
18 Memorandum by Amery for the Defence Committee, 27 May 1943, DO (43) 12, *Ibid.*
19 Howard, *Grand Strategy*, IV, p.543
20 *Ibid.*, pp.544-6; Kirby, *op. cit.*, II, pp.393-4
21 JP (43) 254, quoted in Howard, *Grand Strategy*, IV, p.545
22 Churchill to Ismay, 26 July 1943, PRO, PREM 3, 143/8
23 DO (43) 6, 28 July 1943, PRO, CAB 69. The mention of March 1945 is odd, since the date usually used for planning purposes was December 1944. The latter date appears in a minute from Churchill to Sir Edward Bridges, as early as January 1943 (Churchill, *op. cit.*, IV, pp.928-9
24 Churchill to Ismay, — July 1943, PRO, PREM 3, 143/8
25 *Idem.*
26 Forrest C. Pogue, *George C. Marshall: Organizer of Victory 1943-1945*, New York, 1973, p.200. Embick's anglophobia, like Admiral King's, had developed as a result of his experiences in World War I
27 Joint Staff Mission cable of 7 August 1943, quoted in Howard, *Grand Strategy*, IV, p.563
28 JP (43) 277, 7 August 1943, PRO, PREM 3, 147/2
29 CCS 301, Memorandum by the US Chiefs of Staff, 8 August 1943, PRO, PREM 3, 147/1
30 Dill to Brooke, 4 October 1942, quoted in Howard, *Grand Strategy*, IV, p.91
31 Sykes, *op. cit.*, pp.439-42, 444
32 Howard, *Grand Strategy*, IV, p.556
33 Churchill to Ismay, 24 July 1943, PRO, PREM 3, 143/8 (printed in Churchill, *op. cit.*, V, p.656)

34   Howard, *Grand Strategy*, IV, p.549

35   Churchill, *op. cit.*, V, p.71

36   Howard, *Grand Strategy*, IV, p.549; Sykes, *op. cit.*, pp.448-50, has an account derived from one of Wingate's sisters, of a conversation aboard the *Queen Mary* between Wingate and Churchill that opened with the Prime Minister pointing out the blemishes on the prose of Wingate's report

37   Howard, *Grand Strategy*, IV, pp.549-50

38   Quoted in *Ibid.*, p.550

39   Lieutenant-General Sir Ian Jacob, interview with the author, 3 June 1976. Sir Ian was at the time assistant military secretary to the War Cabinet

40   Churchill, *op. cit.*, V, p.71

41   Ismay to Churchill, 30 June 1949, Ismay Papers, II/3/162/3, MAC

42   Lieutenant-General Sir Ian Jacob, interview with the author, 3 June 1976

43   Ismay to Churchill, 30 June 1949, Ismay Papers, II/3/162/3, MAC

44   COS (Q) 5, 8 August 1943, PRO, PREM 3, 147/2

45   Howard, *Grand Strategy*, IV, p.574

46   CPS 83, 18 August 1943, PRO, PREM 3, 147/1. Italics mine

47   CCS 319/5, 24 August 1943, printed in Howard, *Grand Strategy*, IV, pp.682-92

48   John Terraine, *The Life and Times of Lord Mountbatten*, London, 1968, p.99; Ismay to Mountbatten, 14 May 1946, Ismay Papers IV/MOU/4 D, MAC

49   Howard, *Grand Strategy*, IV, p.577. Marshall was being diplomatic. He had told the other members of the Joint Chiefs on 28 June that he was determined to avoid British control over 'the means of our aid to China,' Pogue, *op. cit.*, pp.257-8

50   Howard, *Grand Strategy*, IV, pp.577-8 John Ehrman, *Grand Strategy*, V, London, HMSO, 1956, pp.135-48

51   Churchill later recalled this episode for the Defence Committee: DO (44) 3, 19 January 1944, PRO, CAB 69

52   Pogue, *op. cit.*, pp.256-7; Sykes, *op. cit.*, pp.461-2

53   DO (43) 9, 28 September 1943, PRO, CAB 69

54   'Indian Policy: A Memorandum by the Prime Minister and Minister of Defence', 6 October 1943, WP (43) 445, PRO, CAB 66

55   The directive is WP (43) 450 (Revise), 8 October 1943, *Ibid.*

56 Mountbatten's directive is printed in Kirby, *op. cit.*, III, pp.456-7

57 P. Moon (ed.), *Wavell: The Viceroy's Journal*, London, 1973, pp.3-4

58 'India's War Effort', WP (43) 89, 1 March 1943, PRO, CAB 66

59 Memorandum by Amery for the War Cabinet, WP (43) 197, 10 May 1943, *Ibid.*

60 WP (43) 208, 17 May 1943, *Ibid.*

61 This episode is described and analysed in Philip Mason, *op. cit.*, pp.513-14. The troops involved had been affected by the *Kirti Lehar* or 'Peasant Movement', which preached peasant communism. The episode was an isolated one and awakened no response in any other army unit

62 Churchill to Amery, 9 May 1943, PRO, PREM 3, 232/9

63 COS (T) 21, 18 May 1943, *Ibid.*

64 WM (43) 72, 20 May 1943, *Ibid.*

65 Churchill to Amery, 20 June 1943, *Ibid.*

66 Amery to Churchill, 3 August 1943, *Ibid.* See also Auchinleck's letter to Brooke of 9 September 1943 on the same subject in J. Connell, *Auchinleck: A Critical Biography*, London, 1959, pp.755-8. Auchinleck pointed out that the cream of the Indian Army was in the Middle East and that many problems would be eased by their return to India. Nothing came of this as Indian divisions from the Middle East were soon to go to Italy

67 Churchill to Amery, 10 August 1943, PRO, PREM 3, 232/9

68 WP (43) 455, 6 October 1943; WP (43) 450 (Revise), 8 October 1943, PRO, CAB 66

69 Irwin's notes, written after these meetings, are in the Imperial War Museum, Irwin Papers, 2/2, 2/4

70 Kirby, *op. cit.*, II, pp.385-7

71 Hartley to War Office, 19 June 1943, PRO, PREM 3, 232/9

72 COS (43) 215 (Final), 29 July 1943, *Ibid.* There is also a note by Ismay in this collection, dated 30 July 1943, summarizing the discussion to date about reductions in the Indian Army

73 I am grateful to Lieutenant-General Sir Reginald Savory who supplemented for me the material on training found in the official history (letter to the author, 24 October 1976)

74 Kirby, *op. cit.*, III, pp.33-5; Field-Marshal Lord Slim, *Defeat Into Victory* (3rd ed., unabridged), London, 1972, pp.177-80

75 Slim, *op. cit.*, p.164

76 For details see Lewin, *op. cit.*, pp.123-4

77 *Ibid.*, p.127

78 Kirby, *op. cit.*, II, pp.242-3; III, pp.38-40

79 Howard, *Grand Strategy*, IV, pp.553-5; Kirby, *op. cit.*, III, pp.36-40; Connell, *Auchinleck*, pp.743-8; Sykes, *op. cit.*, pp.457-61. The reference to the Indian Army as 'second-rate troops' appears in a paper composed by Wingate at Quebec and quoted by Sykes on p.460

80 J. R. M. Butler, *Grand Strategy*, II, London, HMSO, 1957, p.587; Howard *Grand Strategy*, IV, pp.3-7; Ehrman, *Grand Strategy*, V, pp.41-7

81 Memorandum by Amery for the War Cabinet, 'Morale and the War Against Japan', WP (43) 232, 5 June 1943; Memorandum by A. V. Alexander for the War Cabinet, 'Morale and the War Against Japan', WP (43) 294, 5 July 1943, both in PRO, CAB 66

82 DO (43) 13, 28 June 1943, PRO, CAB 69

83 DO (43) 14, 28 June 1943, *Ibid.*

84 The development during 1942-43 of the Assam line of communications can be followed in Kirby, *op. cit.*, II, pp.50-4, 187-92, 299-301, 366-8, 392-8 489-98; III, pp.17-32, 453-4

Chapter IV

1 Public Record Office (PRO), CAB 69, DO (43) 9, 28 September 1943

2 PRO, PREM 3, 148/1, JP (43) 351 (Final), 6 October 1943

3 Churchill minute, 16 November 1943, PREM 3, 148/1

4 PREM 3, 148/1, JP (43) 351 (Final)

5 Ehrman, *Grand Strategy*, V, p.149

6 *Ibid.*, pp.149-53

7 *Ibid.*, pp.421-5

8 COS minute of 9 October 1943, PREM 3, 148/1

9 On the preliminaries to Cairo I, see Sir John Wheeler-Bennett and A. Nicholls, *The Semblance of Peace*, London, 1972, pp.123-7; Ehrman, *Grand Strategy*, V, pp.155-8

10 Churchill, *op. cit.*, V, p.289; A. Bryant (ed.), *op. cit.*, II, *Triumph in the West*, London, 1959, pp.75-81. See also Ismay to Churchill, 15 June 1949, Ismay Papers II/3/158/3, MAC

11 Ehrman, *Grand Strategy*, V, pp.161-5; Churchill, *op. cit.*, V, pp.290, 294

12 Churchill, *op. cit.*, V, pp:324, 332, 358

13   *Ibid.,* pp.361-5

14   *Ibid.,* pp.365-6. Churchill, who often did not give the replies his minutes had elicited, here paraphrased Mountbatten's reply and printed a post-war War Office note defending SEAC's request. See also Mountbatten to Churchill, 19 January 1944, Ismay Papers, II/3/271/4, MAC

15   Ehrman, *Grand Strategy,* V, pp.183-223

16   Ehrman, *Grand Strategy,* V, pp.421-5; Churchill, *op. cit.,* V, pp.414-15

17   Churchill, *op. cit.,* V, p.504

18   Ehrman, *Grand Strategy,* V, p.425

19   PRO, CAB 69, DO (44) 3, 19 January 1944

20   Ehrman, *Grand Strategy,* V, p.439

21   PRO PREM 3, 232/11, Churchill to Chiefs of Staff, 17 January 1944

22   PRO, CAB 65, WM (44) 74, 9 June 1944

23   Ehrman, *Grand Strategy,* V, pp.433-5

24   PRO, PREM 3, 148/4 SAC (44) 6, 13 February 1944. Wedemeyer, curiously, was General Embick's son-in-law

25   *Idem.*

26   PRO, PREM 3, 148/4, Wedemeyer to Churchill, 15 February 1944

27   Ehrman, *Grand Strategy,* V, pp.436-7. Ehrman, *Grand Strategy,* V, pp. 562-4 analyzes the conflicting estimates of the forces required for 'Culverin'

28   *Ibid.,* pp.450-6

29   Quoted in *ibid.,* p.442. Ehrman reproduces this minute in full, pp.441-4

30   Quoted in *ibid.,* p.446. The bulk of the Chiefs of Staff reply is reproduced on pp.445-8

31   Quoted in *ibid.,* pp.448-9. Ismay's minute to Churchill of 29 April 1944 (reproduced in *ibid.,* pp.566-8) is a good summary outline of the first four months of the controversy

32   *Ibid.,* pp.456-62

33   B. Bond (ed.), *op. cit.,* II, pp.154, 159

34   Quoted in Ehrman, *Grand Strategy,* V, p.490

35   Eden, *op. cit.,* II, pp.461-2, quoting Eden's diary entry for 6 July

36   Bryant (ed.), *op. cit.,* II, p.230, quoting Brooke's diary entry for 6 July. Unfortunately, Lord Moran's diary, at least in its pub-

lished form, is silent from the end of 1943 until August 1944, by which time the argument was virtually over

37 Ehrman, *Grand Strategy*, V, pp.462-84
38 Churchill to Curtin, 12 August 1944, PRO, CAB 69, DO (44) 13, October 1944
39 Curtin to Churchill, 3 September 1944, *idem.*
40 Ehrman, *Grand Strategy*, V, pp.491-3
41 *Ibid.*, pp.493-503
42 Ismay to Pownall, 27 May 1944, Ismay Papers IV/POW/4/2, MAC
43 Bond (ed.), *op. cit.*, II, pp.166-7
44 Bond (ed.), *Chief of Staff*, II, p.133. Further material on the stormy Somerville-Mountbatten relationship can be found on pp.132, 168-9, 175-6, 177-8
45 S. W. Roskill, *The War at Sea*, HMSO, 1954-60, III, pt. I, p.217. Roskill discusses the issue at some length on pp.214-18. Since the text was completed Captain Roskill's *Churchill and the Admirals* (London, 1977) has appeared. His account (pp.251-9) and correspondence with Commander John Somerville has convinced the author that Pownall's judgement, while doubtless reflecting what many, not least at SEAC headquarters, believed at the time cannot stand without considerable qualification
46 Bond (ed.), *op. cit.*, II, pp.166-7, for Pierse's part in Giffard's downfall
47 Pownall to Ismay, 26 April 1944, Ismay Papers, IV/POW/2/1, MAC. Ismay, replying on 27 May, told Pownall: '. . . we at this end have all had the impression for some time past that Washington did not agree with either you or with us about what could, and could not be done in North Burma and were therefore by passing us and pressing their views on their own people.' Ismay Papers, IV/POW/4/2, MAC
48 Butler, *Grand Strategy*, II, pp.251-2, 259, 350-1; Gwyer and Butler, *Grand Strategy*, III, pp.529-33, 562; Ehrman, *Grand Strategy*, V, pp.38-40
49 Romanus and Sunderland, *op. cit.*, I, p.381. Roughly 50 percent of these were non-operational at any one time
50 Combined Chiefs of Staff paper of 26 November 1943, quoted in Ehrman, *Grand Strategy*, V, p.164
51 Kirby, *op. cit.*, II, pp.307-8
52 *Ibid.*, pp.426-35

53   P. Calvocoressi and Guy Wint, *Total War*, London, 1972, pp.800-9; Kirby, *op. cit.*, pp.431-2

54   Kirby, *op. cit.*, III, pp.73-81

55   Lewin, *op. cit.*, pp.155-60; the unabridged edition of Slim, *op. cit.*, pp.223-47, has Slim's own account. See also Kirby, *op. cit.*, III, pp.133-159, and Lieutenant-General Sir Geoffrey Evans, *The Desert and the Jungle*, London, 1959, pp.122-67. Evans, then a brigadier, commanded the defence of the Admin Box

56   Kirby, *op. cit.*, p.512

57   Ehrman, *Grand Strategy*, V, p.406

58   Lewin, *op. cit.*, p.173-5; Ehrman, *Grand Strategy*, V, pp.408-15, 487; Terraine, *op. cit.*, p.109

59   Kirby, *op. cit.*, III, pp.513-15

60   On the Imphal-Kohima battles, see Lewin, *op. cit.*, pp.167-79, 184-9; Slim, *op. cit.*, pp.285-369; Kirby, *op. cit.*, III, pp.187-204, 235-48, 297-312, 329-74

61   Slim, *op. cit.*, p.369

62   These are printed in full in Kirby, *op. cit.*, III, pp.486-92

63   The literature on Chindit II is large and contentious. Essential reading is Sykes, *op. cit.*, and Derek Tulloch, *Wingate in Peace and War*, London, 1972. Major-General Tulloch was Wingate's chief of staff in Chindit II. Kirby, *op. cit.*, III, pp.169-86, 205-23, 279-95, 399-415, 442-6, provides an account that, while not completely satisfactory to Wingate's partisans, is nonetheless as balanced an account as we have to date. The memoirs of two of Wingate's brigade commanders, Michael Calvert, *Prisoners of Hope*, (new ed.), London, 1971, and John Masters, *The Road Past Mandalay*, New York, 1961, provide gripping accounts of Chindit II, while no student of the war in Burma should miss Charlton Ogburn's account of Stilwell's savage misuse of the American LRP unit: *The Marauders*, New York, 1959. The controversial question of Slim's relations with Wingate is discussed in Lewin, *op. cit.*, pp.142-4, 161-5, 179-84

64   Kirby, *op. cit.*, III, pp.445-6. In a letter to the author (19 November 1976), Lieutenant-General Sir Reginald Savory remarked: 'In my opinion any reasonably-trained and well-led infantry could have done all that Wingate did; and better.' Sir Reginald added that he had intervened to prevent stripping the army in India of its best men. Slim's retrospective assessment (*Defeat into Victory*, pp.546-8) was similar: 'This cult of special forces is as sensible as to form a Royal Corps of Tree Climbers and say that no soldier, who

does not wear its green hat with a bunch of oak leaves stuck in it, should be expected to climb a tree.'

65 Ehrman, *Grand Strategy*, V, pp.491-3
66 Slim, *op. cit.*, p.369
67 Kirby, *op. cit.*, IV, p.461. Mountbatten had evidently come out from England with the belief that monsoon campaigning was practicable and necessary – see his account, based on his diary, of a meeting with Slim and his staff on 22 October 1943, in Lewin, *op. cit.*, pp.131-2

Chapter V

1 Churchill, *op. cit.*, VI, p.146
2 *Ibid.*, pp.129-30
3 *Ibid.*, p.137
4 Churchill's account of this episode is in *ibid.*, pp.136-7, and the relevant extracts from the official minutes of the 13 September plenary meeting are in Ehrman, *Grand Strategy*, V, pp.518-19. The minutes of the Combined Chiefs' meeting on the morning of the 14th are in *ibid.*, pp.520-3
5 Ehrman, *Grand Strategy*, V, p.517
6 Churchill, *op. cit.*, VI, p.141
7 Ehrman *Grand Strategy*, V, pp.506-7
8 *Ibid.*, pp.531-3
9 *Ibid.*, pp.41-7, and J. Ehrman, *Grand Strategy*, VI, *October 1944-August 1945*, London, HMSO, 1956, pp.21-4, contain good summaries of Britain's manpower problems
10 L. F. Ellis, *Victory in the West*, London, HMSO, 1962-68, I, p.459; II, pp.142, 158, 369, 380
11 Kirby, *op. cit.*, IV, pp.26-30
12 Ehrman, *Grand Strategy*, VI, pp.167-9
13 *Ibid.* pp.186-7
14 Slim, *op. cit.*, p.385. It is curious that both Giffard and Leese were comparatively ineffective, the former because of a personality clash with Mountbatten, the latter because of a similar problem with Slim – the fate of both a testimony to the dominating characters of Mountbatten and Slim, who got along splendidly with one another
15 B. Bond (ed.), *op. cit.*, II, p.125, diary entry for 14 December 1943
16 Bryant (ed.), *op. cit.*, II, p.323, diary entry of 8 November 1944

17 Slim, *op. cit.*, pp.395-6. Italics mine
18 The evolution of 'Extended Capital' can be followed in Slim, *op. cit.*, pp.373-406. See also Lewin, *op. cit.*, pp.209-22, and Kirby, *op. cit.*, IV, pp.163-9
19 Ehrman, *Grand Strategy*, VI, pp.179-81; Slim, *op. cit.*, p.396
20 Bond (ed.), *op. cit.*, II, pp.196, 197, diary entries of 1, 17 December 1944
21 Lewin, *op. cit.*, p.210
22 Quoted in Ehrman, *Grand Strategy*, VI, p.182
23 Bryant (ed.), *op. cit.*, II, p.382, diary entry for 17 January
24 Ehrman, *Grand Strategy*, VI, pp.183-4
25 *Ibid.*, p.189
26 *Ibid.*, pp.193-7. The Prime Minister's 30 March appeal to Marshall is in Churchill, *op. cit.*, VI, p.618. There is no reference to this episode in Brooke's published diaries
27 Ehrman, *Grand Strategy*, VI, pp.198-201
28 John Masters, *The Road Past Mandalay*, pp.306-7

Chapter VI

1 These developments may be followed in Ehrman, *Grand Strategy*, VI, pp.220-35, 260, 263-73, 295-99, 347
2 When 'Zipper' was finally mounted, the 23rd Indian Division, with the ill-luck that dogged SEAC to the very end, was deposited on beaches from which deployment against determined opposition would have been nearly impossible, so perhaps it was just as well that it was 9 September and the war over for a week. Kirby, *op. cit.*, V, pp.267-71
3 Ehrman, *Grand Strategy*, VI, pp.249-52; Bryant (ed.), *op. cit.*, II, p.353, diary entries of 24 May, 11, 19, 20 June 1945; Kirby, *op. cit.*, V, pp.83-92. There is considerable evidence that the mood and morale of the remaining British troops in SEAC was so powerfully affected by the ending of the German war that their keenness for further operations was questionable. Private information
4 Ehrman, *Grand Strategy*, VI, pp.248-9, 252-4
5 Slim, *op. cit.*, p.534
6 Nor was there any way in which the British could use the American fixation on China as a lever, although in a moment of extreme irritation Pownall told his diary 'we have something of a lever if we wanted, or had the courage, to use it for all support of US forces here and in China flows through India. We *could* put on

a stranglehold, or threaten to do so, if we felt that way.' But such a violent breach in alliance amity would never have been considered for a moment in London. Bond (ed.), *op. cit.*, II, p.197, diary entry of 17 December 1944

7   Kirby, *op. cit.*, V, p.483. The pipeline carried some 60,000 tons, April-October 1945

8   Lewin, *op. cit.*, p.128

9   M. Gilbert, *Winston S. Churchill*, V, *1922-1939*, London, 1976, p.886, Churchill to Linlithgow, 3 November 1937

BIBLIOGRAPHY

UNPUBLISHED SOURCES

Papers of Lieutenant-General Sir Ian Jacob, GBE, CB: Diary of the Casablanca Conference.
Liddell Hart Centre for Military Archives, King's College, London: Ismay Papers.
Imperial War Museum; London: Irwin Papers.

Public Record Office, London:

CAB 65, 66:	War Cabinet Minutes and Memoranda.
CAB 69:	Defence Committee Minutes and Memoranda.
PREM 3, 143:	Papers relating to Burma, 1943.
147:	Papers relating to Burma, 1943.
148:	Papers relating to Burma, 1944.
232/9, 10, 11:	Papers relating to the Indian Army.

OFFICIAL HISTORIES

British

BUTLER, J. R. M.: *Grand Strategy II: September 1939-June 1941*, London, HMSO, 1957.

EHRMAN, J.: *Grand Strategy V: August 1943-September 1944*, London, HMSO, 1957.

———: *Grand Strategy VI: October 1944-August 1945*, London, HMSO, 1957.

ELLIS, L. F. *et al*: *Victory in the West* (2 vols.), London, HMSO, 1962-68.

GWYER, J. M. A. and BUTLER, J. R. M.: *Grand Strategy III: June 1941-August 1942* (one volume in two parts), London, HMSO, 1964.

HOWARD, M.: *Grand Strategy IV: August 1942-September 1943*, London, HMSO, 1970.

KIRBY, S. W. *et al*: *The War Against Japan* (5 vols.), London, HMSO, 1957-1969.

Bibliography

ROSKILL, S. W.: *The War at Sea, III: The Offensive* (one volume in two parts), London, HMSO, 1960.

WOODWARD, E. L.: *British Foreign Policy in the Second World War I*, London, HMSO, 1970.

Indian

PRASAD, Sri Nandan: *The Expansion of the Armed Forces and Defence Organization*, Calcutta, Combined Inter-Services Historical Section India and Pakistan, 1956.

PRASAD, B. (ed.): *The Retreat from Burma 1941-42*, Combined Inter-Services Historical Section India and Pakistan, 1954.

PRASAD, S. N., BHARGAVA, K. D. and KHERA, P. N.: *The Reconquest of Burma I: June 1942-June 1944*, Calcutta, Combined Inter-Services Historical Section India and Pakistan, 1958.

KHERA, P. N. and PRASAD, S. N.: *The Reconquest of Burma II: June 1944-August 1945*, Calcutta, Combined Inter-Services Historical Section India and Pakistan, 1959.

American

ROMANUS, Charles and SUNDERLAND, Riley: *Stilwell's Mission to China*, Washington, DC, 1953.

——: *Stilwell's Command Problems*, Washington, DC, 1956.

——: *Time Runs Out in CBI*, Washington, DC, 1959.

General

ASTER, S.: *1939: The Making of the Second World War*, New York, 1973.

BOND, B. (ed.): *Chief of Staff: The Diaries of Lieutenant-General Sir Henry Pownall* (2 vols.), London, 1972-74.

BRYANT, A.: *The Turn of the Tide 1939-1943: A History of the War Years Based on the Diaries of Field-Marshal Lord Alanbrooke, Chief of the Imperial General Staff*, London, 1957.

——: *Triumph in the West 1943-1946: A History of the War Years Based on the Diaries of Field-Marshal Lord Alanbrooke, Chief of the Imperial General Staff*, London, 1959.

CALLAHAN, R.: *The Worst Disaster: The Fall of Singapore*, Newark, Delaware, 1977.

CALVERT, M.: *Prisoners of Hope* (new ed.), London, 1971.

CALVOCORESSI, P. and WINT, G.: *Total War*, New York, 1972.

Bibliography

CAREW, T.: *The Longest Retreat: The Burma Campaign 1942*, London, 1969.

CHURCHILL, W. S.: *The Second World War* (6 vols.), London, 1948-54.

CLIFFORD, N.: *Retreat from China*, Seattle, Washington, 1967.

CONNELL, J.: *Auchinleck*, London, 1959.

———: *Wavell: The Supreme Commander*, London, 1969.

EDEN, A.: *The Memoirs of Anthony Eden, Earl of Avon: The Reckoning*, London, 1965.

EVANS, G.: *The Desert and the Jungle*, London, 1959.

FEIS, H.: *The China Tangle*, Princeton, New Jersey, 1953.

FERGUSSON, B.: *Beyond the Chindwin*, London, 1945.

———: *The Trumpet in the Hall*, London 1970.

GILBERT, M.: *Winston S. Churchill V: 1922-1939*, London, 1976.

MACKENZIE, C.: *Eastern Epic, I, Defence*, London, 1951.

MAINS, T.: *Retreat from Burma* (paper ed.), London, 1974.

MASON, P.: *A Matter of Honour: An Account of the Indian Army, Its Officers and Men*, London, 1974.

MASTERS, J.: *Bugles and a Tiger*, New York, 1956.

———: *The Road Past Mandalay*, New York, 1961.

MOON, P. (ed.): *Wavell: The Viceroy's Journal*, London, 1973.

NICOLSON, N.: *Alex: The Life of Field-Marshal Alexander of Tunis*, London, 1973.

OGBURN, C.: *The Marauders*, New York, 1959.

PRATT, L.: *East of Malta, West of Suez: Britain's Mediterranean Crisis 1936-1939*, New York, 1975.

ROSKILL, S. W.: *Naval Policy Between the Wars* (2 vols.), London, 1968-76.

———: *Churchill and the Admirals*, London, 1977.

SLIM, Sir W.: *Defeat into Victory* (3rd, unabridged ed.), London, 1972.

SYKES, C.: *Orde Wingate*, New York, 1959.

TERRAINE, J.: *The Life and Times of Lord Mountbatten*, London, 1968.

TUCHMAN, B.: *Stilwell and the American Experience in China 1911-1945*, New York, 1970.

TULLOCH, D.: *Wingate in Peace and War*, London, 1972.

WHEELER-BENNETT, J. W. and NICOLLS, A.: *The Semblance of Peace*, New York, 1972.

WHITE, T. H. (ed.): *The Stilwell Papers*, New York, 1948.

INDEX

COMPILED BY CONAN NICHOLAS

ABDA command, 33-4, 40, 41, 50, 77, 91, 127
Abyssinia, 17
Admiralty, 13, 15, 16-17, 40, 41, 50, 77, 127, 129
Afghanistan, 18
Air forces:
British (RAF), 16, 20, 21-2, 28, 29, 35, 36, 46, 57, 59, 60, 65, 110, 114, 137, 145, 146, 154; Bomber Command, 127; Coastal Command, 129; Air Transport Command, 130
Chinese, 26, 27
Indian, 23
Japanese, 36
US, 87; Army Air Force, 38, 46, 56, 74; 10th Air Force, 46; Ferry Command, 46; China Air Task Force, 46, 52, 55; 14th Air Force, 55, 58; No. 1 Air Commandos, 102, 129
Akyab, 44, 48, 58, 59, 61, 62, 66, 72, 75, 78, 81, 90, 108, 109, 113, 147, 148, 155
Alexander, A. V., 103
Alexander, F-M Sir Harold, 35, 36, 37, 42, 45, 112, 121, 125, 136, 144, 146
Allied Land Force, South-East Asia (ALFSEA), 151, 156, 161, 162
America, see US
American Volunteer Group ('Flying Tigers'), 27-8, 29, 32, 36, 37, 38, 46
Amery, Leopold, 60, 64, 67, 70, 71, 77, 84, 87, 94, 95, 96, 103, 116
'Anakim', Operation, 45, 46, 47, 49-50, 52-3, 54, 55, 56, 57, 58, 59, 68, 69, 75
Andaman Islands, 47, 108, 148
Anderson, Sir John, 71
Anglo-American summit meetings, see 'Arcadia', 'Quadrant', 'Trident'
Anglo-French alliance, 17
Anglo-Japanese alliance, abrogated, 13

'Anvil', Plan, 107, 112, 113, 122, 124
Arab Revolt, 64
Arakan, 44, 45, 59, 60, 61, 62, 64, 67, 77, 94, 98, 99, 105, 113, 121, 130, 132, 133, 134, 138, 147, 155
'Arcadia' Conference, Washington, 33, 41, 50, 53, 80
Armies:
Australian, 40
British, 63, 64, 96, 98; 7th Armoured Brigade, 34, 35, 37; 18th Division, 35, 40; IV Corps, 48, 61, 65, 101, 105, 109, 113, 130, 132, 137; XV Corps, 61, 62, 99, 105, 130, 132, 133, 147, 148; 2nd Division, 63; 13th King's Liverpool Regiment, 65; XXX Corps, 84; 70th Division, 102, 103; 11th Army Group, 125, 130, 152; 14th Army, 130, 138, 141, 147, 148, 149, 154, 155; XXXIII Corps, 137, 141, 154, 157
Chinese, 42, 56, 104, 109, 130; Expeditionary Force, 37; Sixth Army, 38, 39; Fifth Army, 39; 66th Army, 39, 47
German, Sixth Army, 137
Indian, 17-20, 22-5, 59, 60, 61, 63, 69, 77-8, 85, 94-9, 100, 101, 103, 106, 125, 130, 133, 147, 159; 4th Division, 18, 20, 22; External Defence Troops, 19, 20; Gurkha Rifles, 20, 65, 101; 14th Division, 59, 60, 61-2, 66; 17th Division, 32, 33, 35, 36, 61, 101, 134, 155, 160; 63rd Infantry Brigade, 35, 36, 60; 39th Division, 61; 77th Infantry Brigade, 65, 66, 101; Army Service Corps, 100; 23rd Division, 98, 101; 7th Division, 101, 132, 133, 135; 20th Division, 101
Indian National Army, 97, 131, 132, 137

Index

187

Index

Index

Mussolini, Benito, 80
Mutaguchi, Japanese Gen Renya,
131, 132, 135, 137, 154
Myitkyina, 66, 109, 150

Naval limitation, 14
Navies :
British (Royal Navy), 16, 20, 88,
114, 122, 126, 129, 143, 146
Indian, 23
Japanese, 119
US, 15
Netherlands East Indies, 57, 162
New Guinea, 141
New Zealand, 14, 17, 21, 22
Noble, Adml Sir Percy, 126
North Africa, 45
North-West Frontier, 18, 22, 23, 60,
147

'Octagon' Conference, Quebec, 143,
144, 149
Okinawa, 161
Old, US Gen W. F., 129, 134
'Overlord', Operation, 80, 82, 91,
107, 112, 113, 122, 124, 129, 136,
151
Owen, Frank, 133

Pacific Ocean, 50, 53, 72, 88, 90, 92,
110, 111, 113, 114, 115, 116, 118,
119, 120, 122, 123, 124, 131, 140,
143, 144, 145, 150, 161
Pacific War Council, 50
Page, Sir Earle, 40
Park, ACM Sir Keith, 152
Pearl Harbour, 75
Pegu, Burma, 36, 160
Percival, Lt-Gen A. E., 33
Persia, 18, 96
Persian Gulf, 43
Phillips, Capt T. S. V., 16
Philippines, 76, 141
Pierse, ACM Sir Richard, 57, 59,
68, 69, 74, 127, 129, 152
'Pigstick', 113
'Plan 21', 130, 131
Portal, ACM Sir Charles, 29, 129
Port Dickinson, 147
Port Swettenham, 147
Potsdam Conference, 162
Pownall, Gen Sir Henry, 16, 17, 96,
120, 121, 124, 125, 126, 127, 151,
152, 153, 155, 157

President of USA, *see* Roosevelt
Prime Minister, *passim*
Prome, Burma, 36
Punjab, 23
Pye, Dr R., 81n, 87

'Quadrant' Conference, Quebec, 32,
80, 81, 82, 84, 88, 89, 90, 92, 96,
105, 106, 110, 121, 138, 149
Queen Mary, SS, 13, 71, 82, 83, 86,
87, 94

Ramgarh, 47, 49, 53
Ramree Island, 72, 75, 78, 79, 90,
108
Ranchi, Bihar, 61
Rangoon, 25, 27, 28, 29, 32, 33, 34,
35, 36, 37, 39, 44, 45, 47, 49, 66,
82, 90, 109, 123, 131, 140, 148,
150, 155, 159, 160
'Ravenous', operation, 59, 66
Rome, 80, 112, 122, 136
Rommel, F-M Erwin, 43, 77
Roosevelt, Franklin D., President of
USA, 15, 16, 27, 28, 34, 38, 40,
41, 42, 49, 52, 54, 55, 56, 74, 75,
83, 111, 112, 113, 134, 144-5,
146, 149, 163, 164
Russia, 18, 72

Savory, Maj-Gen Sir Reginald, 98,
100, 132, 163
'School of Bush Warfare, 29
Scoones, Lt-Gen Geoffrey, 61, 101,
130, 137
Scott, Maj-Gen Bruce, 98
Supreme Headquarters Allied Ex-
peditionary Force (SHAEF), 128
Shan States, 33, 39
'Shingle', 113
Sholto Douglas, ACM Sir W., 86-7
Siam, Gulf of, 44
Sicily, 80, 84
Sikhs, 23
Singapore, 13-14, 16-17, 18, 19, 20,
21, 22, 25, 33, 34, 35, 39, 40, 70,
82, 88, 90, 117, 118, 119, 147,
149, 150
Sittang River, 35, 39
Slim, Gen Sir William, 20, 37, 42,
43, 61, 62, 63, 99, 100, 106, 125,
126, 130, 132, 133, 134, 135, 136,
137, 139, 140, 141, 148, 149, 150,

Index